Chesham
Stories ILLUSTRATED

Wey Lane, by artist Mary Casserley, from a series of gouache paintings
of landmarks in and around the Chilterns. *www.marycasserley.com*

by Peter Hawkes

Dedication

Ray East, 1927–2015

In April 2015, at Chesham Bois Cemetery, I witnessed the burial of an old friend. Out in the sunshine and long grass, with the birds singing, there was something deeply beautiful, peaceful and natural about this laying to rest in the earth. I first met Ray East over twenty years ago, having written him a letter. He was well known as a photographer and local historian, and from his collection he produced an image of my great grandfather on his horse and trap up by Captains Wood. It was the start of a great friendship with this man, 40 years my senior.

I admired Ray for his love of freedom and independence. He was a real old Chesham character who had never been far from home. He tried to drive to London once, but got lost and turned back! He would often arrive at my office on his bicycle to show me his latest photographic finds. When I visited him he would be in his garden full of flowers and produce, or in his shed which was a treasure trove of old artefacts. From an old chest of drawers he gave me a leather-bound shop ledger from 1795. From a hook he gave me a top hat that had belonged to the Lord of the Manor. From his pocket he gave me a silver fob watch and chain.

He had long wanted to see his collection of old photographs published, and so I was glad to include many of them in an ever expanding series of books on old Chesham. From then on, Ray called me 'Peter the Great'! He began to go blind in his later years, but he was a tenacious man with a great humour, and somehow he would find his way into the town centre each day with his trolley. He had loved his camera and darkroom, and had known practically everyone in the High Street, so his old age was tinged with sadness. Many of the photographs in this book were archived by Ray in his retirement, and he sold his complete collection to me some years before his death. It is therefore my privilege to continue his work in this book.

IN CONJUNCTION WITH:

Chesham
MUSEUM

A Community Resource

The Chesham Town Museum Project promoted the idea of a museum between 1992 and 2003, and its members mounted an impressive 38 displays in the library. A museum had been called for since at least 1981. **Chesham Museum** is a community organisation that was founded in 2004 in the old stables of a public house 'The Gamekeeper's Lodge', and operated from 2009 to 2017 at premises in Market Square. The museum was conceived and is maintained, run and financed, completely by local volunteers, and by their joint fund raising activities with the support of local businesses, schools and the wider population. The museum aims to educate people about the rich history of Chesham and its past inhabitants. It is currently raising funds for new premises and one aim of this book is to help towards that end. Go to **www.cheshammuseum.org.uk** to find out more.

CHESHAM
HERITAGE

First published in 2017 by Hawkes Design & Publishing Ltd – *producer of the Chesham Heritage Facebook page.*

Copyright © 2017 Hawkes Design & Publishing Ltd

ISBN: 978-1-9998335-0-3

Contents

Introduction

Although I was born at the north end of Chesham town, I spent most of my childhood up at Ley Hill, where any free time was whiled away most happily when walking in fields and woods, or cycling down narrow lanes to Latimer and the River Chess. I developed a deep appreciation of the natural history and countryside around Chesham.

As a young man, driving along Bois Moor Road, I was enamoured with this semi-rural community between trees and Moor – the brick-built terraced cottages with wooden windows and the long strip of allotment gardens by the river – and so it was here that I bought my first house and began a family. The houses were built in the 1880s and '90s with the coming of the railway, but this was an ancient community. Lord's Mill was mentioned in the Domesday Book of 1086 and the diversion of the river to provide a head of water to power the mill was linked to Lady Elgiva's will, from the year 970 – the earliest written record of Chesham.

Another community dating back to the Middle Saxons was clustered around Chesham's church and watermeadow, and it was here that my forefathers lived and worked, in Church Street, for at least 500 years. So it was to the town that I also looked for work. Whereas home was woods and fields, garden and river, the town was bricks and shops, business dealings and human interaction. Over 20 years I moved my design studio from Chiltern House in Waterside (previously Shackman's, the jewellers), to the old British School House in East Street, to Hector Smith's vacant photographic studio above Chittenden's, to Laceys Yard – domain of the Cox family and their old saddlery business.

In that short time the town has inevitably changed. The general sense of disenchantment has faded, as small houses once rented out for a few hundred pounds now sell for nearly half a million, as wooden windows have been replaced by modern materials, and basic family cars now sit alongside shiny BMWs and Audis. It's Eastern European or Turkish voices that catch the ear, not the old Buckinghamshire accent. These newcomers bring diversity, fresh energy and a cosmopolitan culture. The pressure for housing is unrelenting, met lately with garden infilling and more recently with a plethora of flats crammed into impossible spaces. Chesham is still rough around the edges, with a community spirit that is fiercely independent, but the town centre shops are gradually becoming more upmarket. St Mary's Way pierces the town, louder and busier than ever, and soon HS2 trains may course through nearby at up to 250mph.

The photo collection of Ray East, another Moor-dweller, makes up much of this book, now brought up-to-date with stories and images from local residents, past and present. To set down a social history was my aim, intended in no way to be comprehensive, but to aid in my own understanding of how the town has evolved since the invention of photography, and to investigate in greater detail how it operates today. In doing so, I have learnt much, and have met some wonderful Chesham people.

Peter Hawkes, May 2017

(Two particularly good books on Chesham's ancient history are 'The Book of Chesham' by Clive Birch and 'Lady Elgiva: Her Life and Times' by Arnold Baines.)

1. **Chesham Moor.** The hillside in the background contains cultivation terraces called 'The Balks', made by farmers in medieval times.

Chapter One
Town & Country

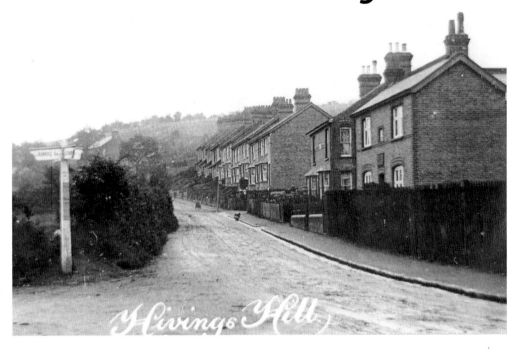

2. to 5. **Then and now.** These photographs from either end of the town – *the foot of Hivings Hill from Bellingdon Road, and Amersham Road from the junction with Amy Lane* – illustrate the transition from country town to suburban commuter town within a century; a change that was inevitable, and the subject of many old Chesham picture postcard books. This new book poses the question: can Chesham retain its unique character as an historic market town with close links to London, or will it slowly succumb to bland urbanisation? I believe that those who care about the town, and understand its story, will work hard to keep the unique identity of Chesham alive.

Views from Dungrove

6. **Old Chesham** by William Butts, c.1900. Although the population of the town has risen threefold since this photograph was taken, the view over the old town remains little changed. The railway station is clearly visible, while Lowndes Park is screened by the avenue of elms.

"The church is a fine old building containing several interesting monuments. Tradition says it is built on a site where originally stood a temple of the Druids." *Souvenir of Chesham postcard c.1905*

"Although mostly modern in appearance, Chesham has been in existence for over a thousand years. The coming of the Metropolitan Railway gave the impetus needed to expand as a residential town and Chesham soon became one of the most favoured parts of what became known as London's 'Metroland'. To retreat from a London office to a home here amid the wooded hills was 'living' indeed." *Chesham Official Guide 1987*

7. **A Chesham Panoramic** taken in the summer of 2008, showing how vital it is to retain our remaining green spaces.

8. **Newtown** c.1920. This industrial area of the town developed during the 19th century, and consisted of factories, workers' cottages, chapels and, later, council housing estates. The buildings of Chesham Brewery can be seen bottom left. The large factory centre right is Webb's brush works. Above and to the right of that is Newton's boot factory. The ecclesiastical building is the United Free Church *(see p38)*.

"Chesham is a thriving little town nestling among the Chiltern Hills and having a population of about 8,000. The chief industries are the manufacture of boots, brushes and woodenware articles." *Souvenir of Chesham postcard, c.1905*

"There is probably no market town within 30 miles of London so picturesque and quaint, combined with such business energy and enterprise, as the town of Chesham. It is reached from the metropolis by the Metropolitan Railway, and lies in a valley or basin almost surrounded by spurs of the famous Chiltern Hills." *G J Smith, 'A Chat About Chesham,' 1903*

9. **Red kites** had been made extinct by gamekeepers in England by the end of the 19th century. Between 1989 and 1994 they were reintroduced to the Chilterns, and this became one of the greatest conservation success stories of the 20th century.

The River Chess

12th century
St Mary's church, after its
restoration in 1867

Rear of
Germain Street with
high brick wall

10. **Amy Mill pond,** off Red Lion Street, photographed some time between 1873 and 1888. This large body of water, once used to power the mill, has now reverted to a mere stream (see below). The Aylesbury ducks in the foreground were bred by locals for the London market and although Waller's of Chartridge still keep this breed today, wild mallard ducks are now more commonly seen on the Chess. With the closure of Amy Mill, this area was used for watercress growing.

11. **At the Meades Water Gardens,** the Town Council converted the disused watercress beds to a pleasure gardens with a small lake in 1979. As it silted up over time, the Chiltern Chalk Streams Project restored the original course of the river in 2008.

Clock tower of the Market Hall, dating from 1856

Sign of the Nag's Head Inn, which dated from 1695

Zion Chapel of 1873, before enlargement in 1888

12. to 14. **Chalk stream wildlife.** Despite the decline in water levels due to low rainfall and over abstraction, the River Chess is a haven for wildlife today. The Chesham Wildlife Facebook Group was set up to enable members to post and view wildlife pictures taken in a 10 mile radius of Chesham. Swans and kingfishers have thrived along the length of the river since living memory, but a relative newcomer is the little egret. Other distinctive wetland birds to look out for are herons, grey wagtails and the great white egret. Watercress and water crowfoot grow prolifically, and Britain's most endangered mammal, the water vole, is conserved locally.

15. **The two-acre millpond of Lord's Mill,** with Moor Road to the right. Note how the road is lower than the water level. This is evidence of the diversion of the river in Saxon times to create a head of water to power the mill, possibly by command of Lady Elgiva prior to the year 970. The original 10th century mill was built by penal slave labour under Brihtric, thegn of Edward the Confessor's Queen Edith.

16. **Listed in the Domesday Book of 1086,** Lord's Mill was the oldest of the mills along the length of the River Chess. It was used for the grinding of corn. The 17th century version of the mill building was demolished in the 1980s. Initially it had two small waterwheels, but these were replaced in the 19th century by a narrow breast-shot wheel of great diameter. This, in turn, gave way in 1900 to a wide undershot wheel within the building, necessitated by the lessening difference between the level of the millpond and the outfall stream. The continuingly reduced flow of the River Chess was one of the factors that caused the mill to convert to steam and then to electric. Prior to closure in 1955 it was the oldest working mill in Buckinghamshire.

"Another mill, lower down the Chess was Channer's. There was a wood merchant's beside it, and a field full of logs. We were told not to go there as they could fall on us, but on a few occasions of course, we did. If we kept very still and quiet we could see a flash of turquoise as a kingfisher darted into the depths of the stream. We could dam the river there too and paddle."

Pam Bayliss (nee Sale-Thorn) — from her story 'A 1940s' Childhood in Waterside'

17. **The buildings of Amy Mill** drawn by H Bates, 1904. As this mill was nearest the source of the River Chess, it was the first to suffer from falling water levels.

Floods, Springs & Watermeadows

19. **Site of the chalybeate spring.** Mineral Cottage in Amersham Road was built in 1821 to enclose a mineral spring that produced waters rich in iron, which were reputed to cure many ills. It accommodated visitors coming to take the waters and Chesham might well have become a prosperous spa town, like Royal Tunbridge Wells, had the spring not failed some years later.

18. **Chesham was known to the Saxons as 'Ceasteleshamm'**, meaning 'pile of stones by the water meadow' – probably referring to the pudding stones in St Mary's Church by this riverside area. These two ladies are standing on what is now the site of Watermeadow car park.

21. **Aftermath of the flood in Church Street.** On 17th May 1918 there occurred the worst recorded flooding in Chesham, following a cloudburst along the Pednor Valley. Water at least three feet deep reached Pednormead End – pictured here by The Bell beershop – and inundated houses in Church Street, Wey Lane, Germain Street and beyond with mud, water and debris. Legend has it that the author's Uncle Reg was chased the length of Pednor (then also known as Frogmoor) by the bow wave, back to his house at 80 Church Street. A substantial clean-up operation ensued after the flood.

20. **Vale Road** has always flooded, as the Vale Brook feeds into the River Chess from the fields above, and into the valley.

A Market Town

22. **The Old Berkeley Hunt** passing through Market Square. A Market House was first mentioned in 1679, when the area was most likely used as a cattle and sheep market. Livestock was later moved across the road to Nag's Head Yard and the building was enlarged in 1856 by Lord Chesham for use as a corn exchange, where dealers in corn could set up their stands and exhibit their offerings. After 1870 the flood of cheap corn from North America made this purpose obsolete, and it came to be used as a Town Hall and venue for theatre, cinema and gatherings. The bell seen in the clock tower was rung at 12 o'clock on Wednesdays to denote the opening of the market. It also originally served to give alarms of fire. It dates from 1748 and has recently been reintroduced to Market Square to strike the daytime hours.

"There was a cattle market in the High Street and Broadway on Wednesdays. Farmers came in from the surrounding farms. They brought business into the town and ate in the local eating places. Before buses, horse-drawn carriers brought villagers into town and goods out.

A lot of people from Townfield Yard were moved up to Pond Park. They were all very poor people. We used to run up the steps; we daren't walk in case the people came out, we were afraid of them. They keep building up there; it was just a hill then."

Mrs Checkley, interviewed at the Deansway nursing home around 1982 by three Brushwood School pupils.
She was 90 at the time, so born c. 1892

23. **The rise of the motor car and the decline of the market.** A pair of Mark 1 Ford Cortinas date this photograph to the early 1960s, when cars had begun to radically change the face of the town. As the Town Hall fell into disrepair, the clock tower was removed.

24. **The Market Square in 1965.** This space, first laid out for the market in 1257, had now lost its central building. The motor car was king, and the way was clear for the construction of St Mary's Way. The Co-operative record shop is revealed, signalling a new era of electronic pop culture – a blend of music, fashion, radio, film and television – driven by a younger society and an affluent generation.

25. **Opening of St Mary's Way,** 1968.

"Councillor Bill Sills, Chairman of Chesham Urban District Council, liberated the town from the bonds of rush hour traffic jams and High Street hold-ups. Councillor Sills cut the ribbon to let through a convoy of special guests and councillors in a Rolls Royce ... hotly pursued by a stream of youngsters on cycles. Police were soon getting complaints from pedestrians, who were finding it difficult to cross roads in the new system." *The Bucks Examiner*

Return of the Market

26. and 27. **Discovery of the old Darvell's bread oven,** 1989. During the demolition of part of Church Street to extend and widen St Mary's Way, this baker's oven was uncovered at No.14. The business was established in 1838 by William & Sarah Darvell and still operates today in the High Street. By allowing two-way traffic to bypass the Market Square, the town centre could be pedestrianised.

28. **The new clock tower.** A crowd gathers on Saturday 17th October 1992, to watch the mayor, Andrew Ketteringham, climb the ladder to start the clock at 12 noon. It stopped shortly after the ceremony and had to be restarted!

29. **The local produce market,** back in its rightful place in Market Square, 2017.

Chapter Two
Childhood

30. and 31. **In 100 years the lives of local children have been transformed beyond recognition.** They have access to vastly improved healthcare, education, information and entertainment. They can connect with each other and play in virtual reality using computer technology, but have perhaps lost much of their connection with the natural world. However, research indicates that traditional playground culture and children's games are not overwhelmed, marginalised or threatened by the new media.

32. and 33. **Town and country children,** in the High Street c.1910 and below Hill Farm, 1998. Children once made their own games in town, playing with locally made wooden hoops or marbles. Out in the country, boys often hunted for birds nests. The quality of entertainment has much improved, although the freedom to roam has been curtailed!

Birth

"Our birthdays were never celebrated, and we never had any presents, or even a card. In fact, until my school teacher told me differently, I had thought my birthday was on the 12th April. I was informed rather frostily that "Hilda Birch, your birthday is the 13th, not the 12th." The only time I remember getting a present was when I had a Sunday school teacher named Mr Bunker. He knew when my birthday was and would bring me some chocolate and leave it with mother. I would rush home from school on my birthday asking: 'Has Mr Bunker been yet, Mum?' Luckily for me he always had."

Hilda Jane Brown (1905-2000)

"My mother left me in my pram outside Chesham Post Office in 1957 and caught the Rover bus home. She'd just made a cup of tea when she remembered and a neighbour took her back to collect me. I was fine and no-one had noticed!"

Lyn McCulloch Fegan (née Lynda Whyte of Ley Hill), 2017

34. **A Victorian perambulator or 'pram'.** The ornate fashion of the era made most products look like works of art.

35. **Grocery shopping, 1960s.** Remarkably, it was common practice in those relatively safe and trusting days to leave babies outside in their prams unattended, whilst the mothers did their shopping. The Silver Cross was established as Britain's premier pram manufacturer during this era. By the 1970s, however, the trend was towards a more basic design with a detachable body known as a 'carrycot'. Now, prams are very rarely used, being large and expensive when compared with push chairs, which have been popular since the 1980s.

At Play

36. **Children playing on the Upper Moor** c.1895. According to Daisy Rose Hunt (née Puddephatt, 1920), children often played hoop, top, skipping and hopscotch. With the boys they played rough and tumble football, as well as cricket. They would pick mushrooms when the fields were fresh with dew, and also played in the fields and woods, climbing trees and swinging out on the boughs.

37. **Moor Road** c.1900. A family walking by the River Chess next to 'The Island'. Island House is near the junction with Amersham Road.

38. **Moor Road** 1956. Ann and Janet Cottington feeding the ducks beyond the railway bridge.

"In winter, Trapps Lane became our focus. Armed with an old tin tray we would make a slide down the lane. It was treacherous. One day the vicar who lived in the Rectory above Christchurch came out of his house ready for Evensong. He was clad in his black cassock and cape. He smiled at us, as he stepped right onto our slide! With a cry he hurtled down the hill, cape and cassock billowing out behind him."

Pam Bayliss (née Sale-Thorn) – from her story 'A 1940s' Childhood in Waterside'

"During the school holidays we had to make our own entertainment. Often we would go camping at Big Round Green. We did not have real tents; all we had was old sacking put together with string. Once we had a bad thunderstorm and ran home wet through at two in the morning."

Maurice Payne, born 1913 in Blucher Street

Celebrations

39. The coronation of King George VI and Queen Elizabeth, celebrated in Chesham, May 1937.

"There was a parade from Lowndes Park down to the football meadow where a fête was held. A pencil manufacturer in Bellindgon Road made a propelling pencil with the King and Queen's faces on and a crown as the propelling part. One of these was given to every school child in Chesham." *Ron How, in his book 'Christmas to Anytime'*

QUEEN VICTORIA COMES TO CHESHAM, JULY 1841

"As soon as the cavalcade appeared on the hill above the valley of Chesham, the cannon posted on the opposite hill commenced firing a double royal salute of half-minute guns. At the entrance of the town, her Majesty was received by the Chesham troop of Bucks Hussars, under the command of Captain Fuller; by whom, with a large body of horsemen, she was conducted to Great Berkhampstead. On entering Chesham, her Majesty's carriage slackened speed to a steady walk at which pace it proceeded through the whole length of the town, and through the four triumphal arches which had been erected at various parts. One of the most imposing and affecting parts of the whole pageant consisted of the Sunday School children, to the number of 850, who had been collected in a long row of waggons in the Broadway, and from whom there issued a shout of little voices and a clapping of hands quite overwhelming." *Reverend Charles Lowndes (1808-1890)*

40. Children gathered to greet the return of Lord Chesham *(below)* at the end of the Second Boer War, 1902. Charles Cavendish was Major General of the Imperial Yeomanry in South Africa. He died in 1907 after a fox-hunting accident, when he was thrown from his horse.

41. **Victory party,** Springfield Road, 1945. Mrs Brownsell is wearing the hat *(left)*, Henry Stone stands centrally, and Mrs Connell is to the extreme right.

42. **The first Schools of Chesham Carnival, 1974,** with founder David Steel, special guest Terry Wogan, and Frank Massa of Thomas Harding School PTA. Another famous special guest was Diana Dors.

43. **An Essex Road / Brockhurst Road** mid-century street party and pram race. The sweet shop of Fred Barnes on the corner of the two roads is currently Woodley's Plumbing & Heating.

44. **The Schools of Chesham Carnival** in its third year, 1976. The theme on this occasion was 'Planet of the Apes' and some of the costumes reportedly traumatised the young audience!

"David Steel [1938-2012] and his young wife Linda chose Chesham as a better place to raise a family than London, and they moved out in 1965 to Waterside. They loved the fact that Chesham presented such good activities and schools. Within a few short years their family had grown to five. David was not one to take without giving back and he felt an urge to help improve the schools and the town. His first contribution was born after watching a pram race. Seeing how the people of Chesham came out to support such an event, and how much fun they were having, he had soon convinced a group of locals and like-minded parents to form The Schools of Chesham Carnival committee. In 1974, to the theme of Alice In Wonderland, Chesham had it's Carnival. The event was a huge success. It was opened by Radio One DJ Terry Wogan and literally thousands of people converged on the Moor, where the early Carnivals took place." *Glenn Steel*

School Days

45. **The Board School,** Townsend Road, opened in 1878 when the British School (1828) and the National School (1845) were overflowing with children from the new factory workers' cottages of Newtown. These boys (note their hobnailed boots) might first have learned to write their letters in sand trays and, when about seven, have progressed to writing on slates with a slate pencil.

"When I was nine years old, I attended the British School, at Chesham and one day I saw four or five men go into the village shop, and buy some brass wire. I guessed what they wanted it for, though they little thought that a pair of sharp eyes were watching their movements. The men came out of the shop, and went off by Mr Fuller's place ... I at once informed Mr Fuller of what I had seen."

John Wilkins in 'The Autobiography of an English Gamekeeper', 1892

46. **Whitehill School** opened in November 1890, a few days after the closure of the old British School in Townfield Yard. The Headmaster of the Boys' Department from 1895 to 1929 was Mr Stephen Dodd (back left), and his deputy was Mr Edward Culverhouse (back right). Note the Victorian fashion for dressing children in sailor suits and 'Little Lord Fauntleroy' lace collars. In this turn of the century image, pencils and paper are now in evidence, instead of the old slate pencils.

47. **Infant boys and girls** were taught together at Newtown School, which opened in 1932, although they arrived via separate entrances.

48. **Needlework** was taught to senior girls at Whitehill School in the 1930s. Boys and girls were kept strictly apart.

"In 1932 a brand new Newtown Infants School awaited me. As well as Newtown, junior girls went to Townsend Road School, junior boys to Whitehill School, which also accommodated senior girls on another floor, and senior boys went to Germain Street School. I was fascinated by Newtown School. I remember the pastel coloured classroom walls, and the brightly coloured pictorial alphabet which decorated them. The desks and chairs were small size to fit small figures, as were the toilets and racks of pegs for outside coats." *Joyce Page, born in Bellingdon village in 1928*

49. and 50. **The development of Waterside's schools** mirrors that of most local primary schools in the second half of the 20th century. With the population of Chesham rising from less than 9,000 in 1931 to over 20,000 in 1971, the smaller schools, such as this one *(left)* at Chessmount, were demolished or enlarged to become 'combined' schools for pupils aged 4 to 12.

51. **Whitehill School closed in 1967,** the year that the Plowden Report recommended sweeping changes to primary education in England. The junior boys moved to Thomas Harding and the junior girls to Brushwood. Chesham Preparatory School, est. 1938, provided an independent alternative.

52. **Senior boys** after completion of 'O'-levels, on their last day at Germain Street School in 1964.

53. The Young Enterprise charity was founded in the USA in 1962 and came to the UK in 1973. It reached Chesham in 1976 when 28 young people from local schools and colleges experienced the setting up of a company for one year, which they called Chesscom. It was the subject of a BBC2 documentary film 'Focus on Work'. In this photograph, Vanessa Gilbert *(above, right)* from Lowndes School, helps oversee a Christmas cracker production line. Young Enterprise is still thriving today.

"I think one of the best things about Chesham High was that boys and girls were completely equal."
A past pupil, interviewed for 'Chesham Town Talk' magazine in 2007

54. Partial demolition of Townsend Road School in 1989. After more than 120 years, the fabric of this school could no longer meet educational demands. A remaining part of the building is currently the Citizens Advice Bureau.

55. to 58. From Technical to Grammar. Opened in 1947 at the top of White Hill, with just two masters and six boys, Chesham Technical School taught trades such as plumbing, carpentry and brickwork, a result of the Education Act of 1944 which set up the tripartite arrangement of grammar, technical and secondary modern schools. In the 1960s it was renamed Chesham Technical High School as it became a co-educational grammar school. A further rename to Chesham High School occurred in 1970 as it moved further away from its technical roots, and then to Chesham Grammar School in 2010. There are currently about 1,200 male and female pupils, including nearly 350 in the sixth form. Pictured is Ann Cottington in her 1962 school uniform, and as part of the school hockey team. Buckinghamshire resisted the national move towards comprehensive education in the mid-1960s and has retained the selective secondary school system. Those not passing the 11+ test were offered Lowndes or Cestreham schools in Chesham.

59. Secondary Modern. Chesham Park school was formed in 1988 by merging Cestreham Boys' School and Lowndes Girls' School. It was renamed Chesham Park Community College in 1993 and Chiltern Hills Academy in 2011, with specialist status for performing arts and design. Pictured is the state-of-the art atrium space.

Chapter Three
Finding work

60. to 65. **Chesham at work.** Prior to the industrial revolution that began in the late 18th century, Chesham's trades were connected to agriculture, or related to its by-products. Most numerous were the tanners, leather curriers and shoemakers. Then there were the wheelwrights, smiths and ploughwrights. Alongside them were millers, maltsters, potters, woodenware workers and straw plaitters.

Then, in the 19th century, cottage industries grew to become major factory-based enterprises. Chesham became known as the town of the four 'B's – beer, brushes, Baptists and boots! A fifth 'B' has been suggested – bricks – to include the numerous brick kilns in the villages around the town.

Factories were a great source of employment, some providing work for 50 or more. Hours were long – from 7 or 8 o'clock in the morning to 6 o'clock in the evening and the work was hard. Half day was on Saturday and pay day was Friday, when wives would wait outside the premises in the evening to pick up the wages from their husbands, before they had a chance to spend their earnings in one of the many pubs.

Pictured above are just a few of the hundreds of diverse products made in Chesham during the 20th century: flags, teddy bears, handbags, aluminium foil, medical ventilators and matting. The story of 'Chesham at Work in the 20th Century' has been told in a previous book. Find out on pages 26 to 28 what became of the old factories.

66. **Unlike the factory workers,** bankers, lawyers and office staff, in their ivory towers, seem to have generally escaped the camera!

A Farmer's Life

67. **J Newman of Nashleigh Farm.** This tranquil scene belies the state of almost continual crisis that the average farmer faced in rapidly changing times. Vastly cheaper wheat from America, and meat from Australia and New Zealand, came to Britain by steam ship in the 1890s, forcing many farmers to focus on milk production for local towns and villages, and which could also be sent by train to London. Nashleigh Farm, which is situated along the Ashley Green Road, stopped being a working farm in the 1930s. The farmhouse fell into disrepair but was restored in 1938 as a private residence. The pond, woodland and grazing land remains.

"When Tony Harman took on Grove Farm in Chesham, in 1931, he milked his 18 cows by hand and sold the produce to people in villages nearby. He farmed his 150 acres using methods that had hardly changed in 150 years. Now, from the same farm, he and his son manage 800 acres using the latest equipment and have exported their pedigree beef cattle all over the world.

In the intervening years there have been more changes in farming than at any time since the Middle Ages. Tony has seen the horse-drawn binder give way to the combine harvester. His yields of wheat have risen from 18 cwt per acre to as much as 80 cwt. And his local area has changed from a placid rural community to a busy commuter suburb."

An introduction to Tony Harman's book 'Seventy Summers' that became a BBC TV-series in 1986. His grandson now runs the farm.

68. **Fred Channer of Halfway House Farm,** with a tethered bull outside his farm house on the Missenden Road in 1957/8. The bull was called 'Winchendon Precious Defender'! The extended Channer family held several farms around Chesham and at one time ran the dairy shop in Chesham Broadway.

70. **The courtyard of Pednor House** has the upper road running through it. The old farm house dates from the 17th century, but there have been many ornate embellishments. It was purchased by an American in the 1920s, who proposed to demolish it and re-erect it back home. The great financial crash of 1929 put an end to that idea, but the 15th century Sun Inn, Church Street, was rebuilt brick-by-brick in Flecridge, Pednor by another developer in 1936.

69. **Pednor Bottom.** Mr Pearce enjoys the view in August 1931. Pednor is made up of several small farms and some grander dwellings, including Sear's Barn, Pednor Mead Farm, Bury Farm and Little Pednor Farm. Much of the land was used for cattle and wheat 50 years ago, but is now mostly rented out for sheep grazing. There has also been an increase in horse grazing and equestrian activities. A number of springs that source the River Chess lie along this valley bottom.

71. **Herbert's Hole, Pednor.** In the summer of 2016 this was the most photographed view in Chesham. Situated just on the outskirts of town, the fields are part of an Area of Outstanding Natural Beauty. The poppies grow along Herbert's Hole (once pronounced 'Arbersawl' in a broad Bucks accent), a path which leads to the village of Ballinger.
These days the 'Pednor Loop' is a favourite 5-mile road route for cyclists, walkers and joggers who wish to avoid the town's traffic.

Factory & Trade

72. **The industrial revolution,** In the second half of the 18th century, brought many people from the countryside into the towns, where they could make more money working in the factories. The availability of local timber contributed greatly to the importance of Chesham as a centre for the woodenware trade. The Wright family were working with wood from the 1860s onwards and by 1905 Jesse Wright was operating from this factory in Berkhampstead Road.

73. and 74. **Peter Sadler's paintings** show James East's wood yard in Albany Place, Broad Street *(top)* and the interior of Jesse Wright's factory with its steam furnace.

75. **The front of Jesse Wright's woodenware factory,** Berkhampstead Road. Graham Benwell of Sunnyside Road is outside on his bicycle in the early 1960s, by which time the business had closed. It had been a major employer in the town, making all manner of specialist items from malt shovels to polo balls. The factory was soon after demolished and the chimney dismantled brick by brick.

76. **The site of Wright's factory** is now Chesham's Healthzone, known as the Chess Medical Centre since it opened in 2011.

77. and 78. **Water Lane** off Germain Street, was the site of another wood yard belonging to the Wright family. In the 1870s William Wright was known for his cricket bats, trundle hoops, toy spades, spoons, bowls and butter prints. Two students from the Technical College are seen sketching the factory in the early 1960s, shortly before it was demolished. The second photo shows the site prior to Watermeadow car park.

79. **Rear of Webb Jarratt's brush factory,** Townsend Road, 1983. Founded in 1829, Webb's was a traditional brush manufacturer. In 1897 this much larger factory was built in Townsend Road to develop the mechanised side of brush making and new machines were constructed within these premises. Brushes were made for such diverse requirements as road sweeping, for the dairy, for vacuum cleaners and for cleaning barnacles from ships' hulls. The business finished in 1983 owing to the changing economic climate and the strength of foreign competition.

80. **Opening of Great Mills,** August 1984. The Webb Jarratt factory was demolished and this DIY retail warehouse was built in its place, creating 30 new jobs. It later became a Focus store, and is currently a branch of Wickes. Known to generations of Chesham school children as 'Parrygarrick', the footpath in the foreground was once the site of the town's end, where the hamlet of Bellingdon came down to Chesham. Before Albany car park was built, three cottages stood here opposite East's Woodenware, sited near Parrotts Meadow *(see opposite page, top right)*.

81. **Britannia Boot & Shoe Works** in Addison Road *(above)*. The Renault 8 parked outside dates this photograph to the early 1960s. The factory was built by George Barnes in 1899, and heavy boots were made for farmers, soldiers and coal miners. Despite a serious fire in 1968 it lasted a further twenty years before demolition.

82. and 83. **John Hayes' Boot Factory** in Waterside *(top left)* also dating from the 1890s, was the site of heavy boot manufacture until the 1930s, after which it became a print works. The building fell into decline through disuse from 2003, but fortunately it was bought by Joanna and Nigel Hill in 2010. They made extensive restorations, including a beautiful light, contemporary interior, before opening the ground-breaking Bagnall Centre for Integrated Healthcare in 2012 *(pictured, left)*.

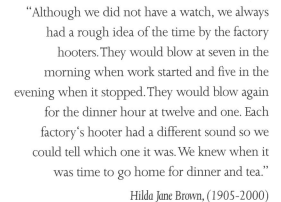

"Although we did not have a watch, we always had a rough idea of the time by the factory hooters. They would blow at seven in the morning when work started and five in the evening when it stopped. They would blow again for the dinner hour at twelve and one. Each factory's hooter had a different sound so we could tell which one it was. We knew when it was time to go home for dinner and tea."

Hilda Jane Brown, (1905-2000)

84. **Asheridge Road industrial estate** pictured in the late 1990s. Most of the town's larger sites are now used for service industries rather than manufacturing.

85. and 86. **The Atlas Pencil Factory** in Bellingdon Road, as seen from Deansway in the early 1960s. The building dated from the 1940s. The factory specialised in making the lead inserts for pencils. It was demolished in the 1970s and is now the site of Atlas House sheltered housing.

Chapter Four
Making a Home

87. **The Pearce family of Chesham,** builders, 1890. Charles Pearce (with bowler hat) ran a family business. He died aged 78 in 1926.

"Over the two decades that I renovated our house at Florence Villas in Lower Bois, I often imagined the skilled builders and craftsmen who had laid the brickwork so immaculately, and joined the old pine timbers of the fire surrounds and dresser so well that they had lasted since 1890. Even the sash windows and panel doors still operated after well over 100 years. I have always loved the solid stonework, the decorative chimney pots and ropework tiles. The men that I saw in my mind's eye looked just like those in this photograph!"

Peter Hawkes, 2017

88. **Houses built in the 1920s by Jesse Mead Ltd** at the far end of Bois Moor Road.

89. **Prefabricated houses** were built at Chessmount in 1943, but these were short-lived. The Willesden Self-Build Housing Group of 1953 allowed people to come out of London and build their own quality homes in Hampden and Berkeley Avenues, using their own labour.

Ancient Cottages

90. Semi-derelict cottages in Townfield Yard.

These old dwellings, along with others in Duck Alley, Parsonage Lane and Waterside, were demolished as part of the slum clearances of the early 1930s. In 1938 a 'model village of residences for old people' called Townfield, off East Street, was designed in their place.

The original residents, however, were removed to the new Pond Park estate, which was initially devoid of community amenities.

"Townfield Yard in the 1920s: Our house was very small. There was a main living room with a solid fuel cooker, the only means of warmth, boiling water and cooking. There was a small wash room at the back. Water was obtained from an outside tap and this and the outside toilet were shared with two other families. The only lighting was by means of oil lamps.

There were not many shops in the Yard. If you were short of bread you could purchase a loaf at the White Lion Inn. The baker, the milkman and a man who sold paraffin all called regularly. We also had occasional visits from a muffin man, a man who sold black puddings, a French onion seller and various 'tally' men trying to sell clothing.

I lived in the Yard for about seven years and in spite of the primitive conditions they were happy ones. I soon got to know all the neighbours; they were mostly kind and friendly people and there were many other children to play with. We were all often referred to as 'backyarders'. This did not bother me; it seemed like a little world of its own."

Lawrence Lacey, born 1915

From Slum Clearances to Council Housing

91. After World War I, large scale provision of working class housing became the responsibility of the state. Chesham's first council houses were built in Brockhurst Road from 1914.

The Pond Park estate followed from 1927. These houses were built in simple cottage style with gabled roofs and horizontal casement windows. They were often rendered or pebble dashed.

No.s 2 & 4 Lyndhurst Road were built in 1928. Herbert & Dorothy Darvell lived at No.2 in 1939, and Mrs Lacey, a widow, and her family lived at No.4. The houses are still standing and fondly remembered.

92. and 93. **Glebe Cottages, New Footpath, off Germain Street,** c.1900.

Mrs E R How is seen here with her daughters, Sarah and Alice, outside their cottage home. The How family were well known for their brewery business in Church Street during the 19th century. Alice *(right)* was the mother of Leonard George Piggin, the town's registrar and local historian for many years.

Vernacular houses such as these were often built with a timber framed construction, and had gabled roofs and casement windows. They were rooted in traditional building techniques and local materials such as brick and flint.

Pictured in April 2017, Amy Deane and Taya are the current tenants at No.1 Glebe Cottages, where Amy has an artist's studio.

"When my mother died in 1973 at No.1 New Footpath – which was my grandfather Charles' home, and to where she moved back after my father died – the house was literally stuffed with old things. I can remember a 4½ gallon barrel marked 'Charles How and Sons' standing in the old washhouse, and am pretty sure that there were old bills and accounts relating to the brewery, but I am afraid that my wife and I had a grand clear-out and the lot went. I was not so much interested in local history in those days!"

L G Piggin, born 1919, and author of 'Tales of Old Chesham,' in a letter to Peter Hawkes, written in 1995

"I love living at Glebe Cottages. The house has great warmth, and there's nothing better than gathering friends and family round the large kitchen table for a home-cooked feast. New Footpath is a peaceful spot and there's great community amongst the neighbours, stopping for a chat and helping each other out. I've often been asked if I'm disturbed by the noise from the school, but I like the sound of children playing, it's vibrant and energetic, and it makes me smile. My dog wags her tail to the sound of the children leaving at the end of the day, and l sometimes let her out to get some fuss. Yes, we're definitely happy here."

Amy Deane, August 2017

Georgian, Victorian & Edwardian

94. and 95. **No.300 Berkhampstead Road,** then and now. From the early 18th century onwards, Georgian houses introduced uniformity and balanced proportions. Sash windows were used, which could be opened without disrupting the symmetry of the façade. 'Rubbing' or 'Windsor' bricks, or plain red stocks, were used for window arches and decorative dressings. The Meades in Germain Street is a fine Georgian house, but lower down the social ranks, smaller homes were built to the same proportions, only on a reduced scale.

96. and 97. **Blucher Street.** No before and after photographs of this terrace can be produced, as it has been completely demolished. The house with its gated front garden, is now the site of Chesham Library, and much of the rest of the street is below St Mary's Way.

98. and 99. **Barnsbury Villas,** built in 1900 (505-511 Waterside). Such high quality terraced housing, with its own name plaque carved in stone, in imitation of larger houses, provided homes for the upwardly mobile, such as artisan workers and clerks. The villas have bay windows, offering more light and space, and better views. The repeal of the Window Tax in 1851 encouraged larger windows such as these.

Victorian front doors tended to have four panels in place of the typical Georgian six panel door. Much use was made of cast iron accessories, fireplaces, railings and gates.

Current owner Gary Wallington outside his family's home in 2017. The first house on the left is considerably bigger as it was owned by the original builder for his own use, and is well preserved. Gary's house was occupied by the Culverhouse family in 1901.

"It was good to meet Gary Wallington who lives along Waterside in these terraced villas. Between 1844 until 1891 another branch of the Wallington family lived at the Rose & Crown public house in Waterside. They were beer retailers and manufacturers of ginger beer and mineral water, and I have an old green glass bottle from Wallington's brewery. James Wallington was the founder, but his widow Ellen continued it into the late Victorian era. Although her step-children Alfred and Sophia seem to have kept it going for a while, it was Arthur and Emily Hawkes who were running the pub by 1911." *Peter Hawkes, 2017*

100. and 101. **130 Broad Street**. Pictured, *left,* is Florence Arnold, née Birch. In the glass above the door behind her is the sign 'T Wilcock's Tailor' and in the window is a free-standing gas lamp. The Victorians loved ornament and embellishment, and these were added to some terraced housing, along with bay windows and moulded brickwork. Such buildings commanded higher rents and pretensions to respectability.

In other streets, speculative builders squeezed many two-up, two-down houses into tightly packed terraces; sometimes back-to-back with very little garden space. Some of these overcrowded and insanitary dwellings were demolished in George Street and Alexander Street as part of the slum clearances right up until 1970. Working class districts had inevitably been built close to the factories which provided employment for their inhabitants. Such mass housing, usually constructed by small scale local builders, still employed local methods and materials. Many of the Victorian and Edwardian streets of Newtown, with their slate roofs, local brick façades and well-designed chimneys and stone features are highly attractive.

102. **The availability of large sheets of glass** resulted in individual panes without glazing bars, requiring heavier timber frames strengthened with mortice & tenon joints at the corners, giving rise to the 'horns' on sash windows *(right)*. The Edwardians designed less ornate houses, and later generations condemned 19th century ornament and manufactured detail. The result is that many period homes were 'modernised' in the post-war decades, with fireplaces ripped out and original doors and windows replaced with ill-fitting alternatives. Thankfully, the current owner of no.130 Broad Street, Christian Schwetz, has seen fit to retain the period features of this home.

"The house at No.130 is still very authentic – the only one in the row that's kept its sash windows, and within it's still largely lime plaster. Funny that the ivy in the photograph is still there. The brick sheds remain at the back that would have been the wash room and WC. There are lots of original plaster mouldings inside and I left the cracks in the ceiling plaster as they look rather characterful!" *Christian Schwetz*

"I devoted 20 years of my life to restoring this house in Bois Moor Road. Many similar houses had their original small rooms knocked through in the 20th century to become open-plan, but this home had retained its cosy back room, panelled in pitch pine, with original dresser and fireplace, dated 1891.

In the 19th century this room would have been used for cooking and eating, with a scullery at the rear for washing clothes, and a toilet outside in the garden. An old cast iron stove must have been ripped out in the early 20th century and substituted with a gas fire, with all fireplaces then panelled over. I re-opened the fireplace and installed a wood burner.

There was no running water in Bois Moor Road until the 1920s and I discovered and excavated an old well in the back garden, restoring it with bricks from H G Matthews and a metal cover made by Cheeld's blacksmiths – two traditional Chesham businesses.

I restored all furnishings, doors and windows to a Victorian design using the services of local carpenters, and even ordered a replacement door number, by copying an original oval design. Many features were restored using reclaimed materials, including a Belfast sink from the Cottage Hospital and old taps re-chromed by Chesham metal finishers, Servex Ltd."

Peter Hawkes, 2017

103. to 105. The author's house in Bois Moor Road. All original features were retained or restored to a Victorian design, and in the garden the old well or catch-pit was rediscovered and made good.

Known as 'Florence Villas', the terrace was built in 1890 – the original occupiers were Joseph Taylor, a boot finisher aged 32, his wife Alice, 27, and their children Harry, 4, and Lydia, 1. Maura Hawkes is pictured outside in 2017, aged 18.

106. The old house identified. This view was photographed long before the building of Cresswell Road and prior to the Iron Mission Room in the foreground being demolished. The River Chess flows to the right, through the allotments of the Duke of Bedford's Trust.

Modern Homes

107. **'Sunningdale', no.7 Bellingdon Road** c.1935, with Mrs Hobbs at the front gate. This 1930s 'Metroland' or 'Tudoresque' style house is typified by the two storey bay surmounted by a gable of barge boards or fake timber framing. There is a return to casement windows and a strong feature is the round-arched open porch with a front door containing stained glass. Many similar houses were built of varying sizes, detached or semi-detached, with a garage to the side to cater for the great rise in car ownership. Many such buildings were rendered or pebble-dashed. Electricity would have been installed from new, alongside all-tiled gas fireplaces. The last owners of No.7 before demolition were Peter and Paula Cabrelli with their children, who moved in from London in 2002.

108. **Liberty Court retirement flats** replaced No.7 to No.15 Bellingdon Road after 2006. UK life expectancy is up 20 years from 1930. Healthier lifestyles and improved medical science means on average a female born today will live to be 82 and a male to 78. In 1930 the equivalent figures were 62 for females and 58 years for males. As well as living longer, men and women are staying healthy and disability free for more of their lives. Accommodation for the elderly is in great demand. (c/o Office for National Statistics)

109. **Uplands Court** c.1960.
A decade after the Second World War there was a decline in the building of semi-detached houses in favour of flats and maisonettes, often on redundant land. Nearby Albany Court was built on the site of Glenthorne House and its extensive gardens.

110. **Gladstone Court** c.1965.
These three storey flats were built on the site of a barn where Chesham Brewery barrels were coopered. Note the large, oblong picture windows and the flat roof unbroken by chimney stacks. Most modern flats were built with full central heating installed.

Chapter Five
Family Values

Genealogy

111. **A typical 19th century Chesham family.** Several generations of each family often lived in the same street or district.

Many surnames in the 1538 Parish Register of St Mary's Church still existed in the town of 1904. Some of the most numerous families of the 16th century had the Saxon-sounding names Birch, Cock, Dell, Gate and Ware. Few people ventured beyond the boundaries of their town and there was inevitably much intermarrying. One curious local name is Puddephatt, an Old English nickname with a Germanic root, meaning 'round and stout', and one unusually early immigrant was Giovanni Sabatini, from Laverno in Italy, who bought nearby land about 1804, and who has many decendants in Chesham today.

The first wave of immigration began in the 1950s and '60s when people from Pakistan, part of the British Commonwealth, were actively encouraged to come to the town to help resolve industrial labour shortages.

112. **Mahnaz Ahmed from Chesham**, pictured in 2003. She studied International Law at Brookes University, Oxford and continues to live in the city, where she has also started a family.

113. **Chesham is over 7% British Pakistani** and 80% white British. Most of the local Asian community came originally from the Mirpur district of Kashmir, in Pakistan, where the language spoken is Urdu.

Religion and Social Strata

114. **A National & Sunday Schools parade,** High Street, representing the Anglican community and St Mary's Parish Church.

116. **The United Free Church Sunday School procession** in Sunnyside Road, c.1907. Chesham is famous for its religious non-conformity, and after a rift with the Baptists, The Reverend Walter Wynn, in top hat, established this new church in Bellingdon Road (now the site of the Methodist Church). Wynn was very ecumenical and made friends with many other church ministers in the town – a precursor to 'Churches Together for Chesham'.

115. **Alfred Chapman and Florence Ing, Daisy Cottage, 46 Severalls Avenue** on their wedding day in 1923. They remained happily together and had two children, Aubrey and Beryl. In 1858 divorce law was introduced in England but divorce remained too expensive and scandalous for most people until the Matrimonial Causes Act of 1923. Currently, 42% of marriages end in divorce.

117. **Religion** in Chesham is diverse, with over 54% percent listing Christian beliefs in the 2011 census. This, of course, can be divided into Church of England, Catholic, Methodist, Baptist and other denominations. Over 8% of the population are Muslim, a proportion recently strengthened by a rise in Turkish residents. Those stating 'no religion' amounted to over 27%.

118. **Prior to the construction of Chesham Mosque,** *(left)* an attractive building opened in 2005, two houses in Bellingdon Road were used for Muslim worship.

In today's relatively classless society, most people have access to television, and may have seen the Vicarage in the TV series 'Midsomer Murders' and the film 'The Imitation Game,' starring Benedict Cumberbatch.

119. and 120. **Gentry, clergy, physicians and lawyers** made up the highest echelons of Chesham society. Pictured at St Mary's Vicarage in the late 1860s, this is likely to be the Reverend Adolphus Aylward and his family. In the Foxells' history of St Mary's Church (2004), the authors propose that the guest pictured may be 'the illustrious Dr Samuel Wilberforce, Lord Bishop of Oxford'.

121. and 122. **Middle classes.** A decidedly affluent-looking Chesham family. It was the traders, factory owners and shopkeepers who made up this broad strata of society. The most successful entrepreneurs owned large properties, such as Broadlands and Glenthorne, which have since been demolished for densely packed flats and houses to accommodate Chesham's burgeoning post-war population.

124. **Gypsies & travellers** lived on the outer edges of society. Many gypsies made an income from selling wooden pegs.

123. **The working classes** at Frederick Racklyeft's boot factory, Higham Road – a scene reminiscent of an L S Lowry painting. The majority of the townspeople would have made up this branch of society from the late-19th to the mid-20th century, when Chesham thrived as an industrial town.

Holidays

125. **The seaside.** In the first half of the 20th century, holidays abroad were quite unthought of by Chesham people, and most of those who went away headed for one of two resorts: Clacton or Southend. Clacton was a great favourite by rail – the return fare was 12 shillings, which included travel on the Underground from Baker Street to Liverpool Street. George Piggin remembered that when walking along the Clacton sea front, it seemed as if about every fourth person was from Chesham. Most of the week was spent on the beach or promenade, and little money was spent. Ice-creams and sweets cost only coppers, and a show at the theatre or band pavilion was only ninepence or a shilling.

126. **The concept of leisure** assumes that people have a certain amount of time, energy and money to spare. In the 19th century, the working classes had little of any of these available. It was not until after the end of the Great War that an annual week off work, with pay, became a person's right. Prior to that, if you wanted time off, you took it without pay. Few did, but made do with the statutory Bank Holidays, which meant that they did not travel very far.

The 1920 Act, bringing in the paid week, meant that Chesham's factories all closed down together, in either the last week in July or the first in August. In the same decade, charabancs and motor buses came into popuar use, which meant that people could be transported as far as the seaside, albeit very slowly. Chesham Brewery, for example, gave employees an annual outing to Brighton by charabanc; there was usually a stop in Windsor Great Park for a picnic lunch.

127. **Town twinning** became established in the UK after the Second World War as a symbol of reconciliation and mutual understanding between nations. Not until 1980 was Chesham twinned with Friedrichsdorf, Germany. Houilles in France was linked in 1986 and Archena in south-east Spain followed in 1995. Chesham Town Twinning Association organises exchanges involving sports people, musicians, singers and other residents of the town who stay in the homes of host families and then entertain them on return visits. Pictured above are local tennis players in Friedrichsdorf. In this century, with worldwide travel and freedom of movement becoming the norm, town twinning has declined in popularity.

128. **A photograph of a Boeing 787** passenger jet flying in front of the moon over Chesham, by local professional photographer Stuart Lloyd. For the Victorian Cheshamite, flying to Ibiza or Magaluf would have been as far fetched as travelling in space! Over the last 40 years, global air travel has increased almost eight fold and is set to continue; bad news for an already heavily polluted atmosphere.

Chapter Six
Transport

129. **Changing times at the junction between Park Road and Blucher Street.** In the 55 years between these two photographs, Chesham's traffic has increased dramatically. In the early 1960s, these were side streets of relative calm. From 1968, St Mary's Way redirected all northbound through traffic around the town, avoiding the High Street. A little over 20 years later it was extended to four lanes to take all traffic north and south through the narrow channel between park and town.

130. **What would a Chesham resident from the early 19th century make of this scene?** They would have already witnessed the industrial revolution and have been familiar with steam engines in factories and on distant railways, but the age of electricity and the combustion engine might seem to them both exhilarating and appalling: tarmacced streets carrying innumerable horseless carriages, rushing at great speeds, past baffling signposts and high poles carrying glaring lights!

Horse Power

131. **A cab-fronted gig** in Broad Street, c.1910. Horse power was harnessed by all branches of society, from the gentry, through working tradesmen, to the travelling gypsies. Although carts and wagons drawn by horses would have been seen in Chesham from Saxon times, passenger vehicles were comparatively rare until the late 1700s.

132. **Horse traps** (open sprung, two-wheeled carts) were particularly popular in the last half of the 19th century. Clearly Chesham's narrow High Street was designed to cater for foot traffic and deliveries by horse. Up until the mid-18th century, the dire state of the roads made travel in such primitively designed vehicles highly uncomfortable. People rarely travelled far.

"My mother, Gladys Francis, née Woodley, remembers the horses being put on Chesham Moor at night for common grazing. She was sometimes allowed to ride them bareback from the Moor to Woodley Hill."

Sue Forey, granddaughter of William Bertie Woodley. Her grandfather was a coal man, and her great grandfather, a drayman

133. **A light two-wheeled trap** driven by G Woodley junior, licensed chimney sweep and carpet beater of Bellingdon Road. He is pictured here on the corner of King Street in 1885. He later ran a removals business from Sunnyside Road. The horse has a single harness with a ridge pad on its back; this supported leather loops which held up the shafts.

134. **A farm cart.** These two wheeled unsprung carts would have been used around Chesham since medieval times. Made to carry raw materials, they needed to be able to tip in order to unload, and required a single medium heavy horse. Note the heavier harness with cart saddle. Horses were used regularly for farm transport up until the 1950s.

135. **A covered wagon** belonging to Mr C G Grace, coal merchant of Bellingdon Road. Two horses are harnessed in tandem and, as the wagon has four wheels, the shafts connected to the horse at the rear are hinged, to allow some vertical play. The bridles have blinkers to go over the horses' eyes, to stop them being frightened by the wheels, as all horses have very good rear vision.

136. **A brewer's dray** outside the Queen's Head public house in Church Street. The dray consisted of a trolley on top of which the beer barrels sat on runners. The horse at the rear, known as the 'wheeler,' has a cart saddle to hold up the shafts on metal chains. Reins were attached to both this horse and the one in front, known as the 'leader'. The driver, standing right, is most likely James Gilbert, drayman for Weller's Brewery. He was born in 1863, and was killed in 1907 when he fell from the dray, leaving his wife with seven children.

Blacksmiths

137. **Gooding's shoeing forge** was run by John Gooding and his sons during the first half of the 20th century. In Chesham and the surrounding villages there were several hundred horses all needing to have their iron shoes regularly replaced, the roads at that time being very rough. He also supplied several large building firms in the town, as in those days much ironwork was needed in the building of a house. The workshop, despite its small frontage, contained three forges (or fires), a furnace and a tyring platform. The buildings at Gooding's were very old, and supported by solid oak beams, many of them originally discarded from St Mary's Church when it was first restored.

138. **Forges were a source of great interest for boys**, who would invariably stand by the open doors to watch the proceedings. To fit a horse shoe, the hoof was held off the floor between the blacksmith's knees, and the nails drawn out of the worn shoe; the hoof was then pared into shape with a sharp knife, the new shoe placed in position, and the nails inserted with a large hammer.

"It was 1940 and the beginning of the Blitz. My father was accountant to Shipman & King, which owned the Embassy cinema. Their head office was based in The Strand but, after a bomb landed on the roof, they decided to evacuate and came to Chesham, housing some staff and our family in the Embassy flats. There was an air raid late one evening and four bombs dropped along Germain Street. Unfortunately, Helen Gooding had been killed. That scare made the staff decide to sleep on mattresses under the balcony at the back of the stalls for a couple of nights."

Iris Lloyd (neé Cannings)

139. **German bombs.** In October 1940 one of the few bombs to land on Chesham badly damaged the house at Gooding's Forge, killing the blacksmith's daughter. The building was later repaired and the forge stayed open into the 1950s.

140. **Olly Ringsell,** pictured about 1900. He lived to the age of 101. S Ringsell & Son ran their smithy at 119 Waterside, under the railway bridge. Their work was in much demand due to the large number of working horses in the area. Chesham, as a country town, was surrounded by woodland where several timber merchants carried on their business. Horses were used for this trade because they were able to drag the timber from the woods where a tractor would get stuck. There were also many farms in the villages, and Chesham was the nearest market town.

141. **Hobbs' forge at No.13 Blucher Street.**
Arthur Hobbs was a farrier (a specialist at shoeing horses who combined blacksmithing and veterinary skills). To make a horse shoe, a piece of iron was cut off from a long bar and put into the fire. The bellows were blown until the metal reached the required heat, then it was taken out with a pair of tongs and hammered on the anvil until half the shape of the shoe was made, and the holes were punched in that side. Following this it was returned to the fire, reheated and the other side treated in the same way. Then back into the fire before the heels and toes were hammered out.

142. **Wallis' forge,** which stood in a yard off the Broadway next to the Congregational Chapel. As motor vehicles came into common use in the 1920s, these shoeing forges turned initially to other work, before closing down altogether. Currently there is only one blacksmith supplying the town and surrounding villages: Stephen Cheeld's of Hawridge Common *(see page 48 for the story of his grandfather's car).*

The Iron Horse

143. **The horsed omnibus to the London & North Western Railway at Berkhamsted.** Until Chesham secured its own railway in 1889, residents were transferred twice daily to Berkhamsted, the nearest rail link to London and Birmingham. By this means, the national daily papers were brought to town each morning just before 11am. Berkhamsted and Watford stations opened in 1837. Prior to the railways, a stagecoach to London operated three days a week from the George Inn, Chesham, arriving at The Bell & Crown, Holborn after a five hour journey; returning the next day. Other carriers by cart or wagon went to The Bell at Warwick Lane, or Smithfield Market.

144. **The 1889 signal box** with its 20 levers went out of service in the '60s but is now preserved.

145. **The Metropolitan Railway** began operations from Chesham in July 1889, to the headline banner of 'Long looked for, come at last'. These early tank locomotives were built for the Underground lines and offered no protection for the crew against the elements. It was originally planned to extend the route to Tring but, when this failed, Chesham became the end of the line. A turntable was then installed to prevent running with the cab first. Now the daily papers could arrive in Chesham by 7.30am. Sixty years later they came on the 5.30am train. (With thanks to 'Chesham Shuttle' by Clive Foxell.)

146. **Station boy, Robert Geary,** collecting luggage in advance from Broad Street residents. He was one of three generations of railway workers in his family.

147. **Through Waterside.** An early GCR tank engine just beyond the originally proposed Moor terminus. Encouraged by Sir Edward Watkin, chair of the Metropolitan Railway, an extra £2,000 was raised by public subscription during the late 1880s to bring Chesham station into the heart of the town – though not before a Railway Hotel had been built in Bois Moor Road, (later called The Unicorn pub and currently Teddies nursery).

148. **The Goods Yard.** At its height, 5,000 tons of freight a month was dealt with. Coal was the main freight inwards, and local goods such as woodenware and watercress were outward bound. Situated between Whitehill School and Chesham Brewery, the site of the Goods Yard and Shed is currently Waitrose car park.

149. **The last steam train out of Chesham,** with a traditional wreath mounted on the smoke bar, on Sunday 11th September 1960. Note the signal box and water tank to the right.

150. **Following electrification,** these aluminium A60 stock were introduced as a 4-car shuttle service from 1962. By the 1980s, the branch line was under threat of closure. Following a hard fought campaign, two bridges in the Waterside area were replaced in 1986, securing the line in time for centenary celebrations three years later.

151. **Station Master, John Hudson,** proudly displaying his station garden. This project was rejuvenated in the 1990s by Barbara Brown and Mark Stephenson, winning several awards.

152. and 153. **Refurbished and in LT livery,** this A60 type train *(left, photographed by the author in 2000)* has recently been replaced by Bombadier S8 stock *(right)*. These new trains, ideal for wheelchair users, necessitated a through service to London, much to the joy of local commuters. 2010 marked the end of the shuttle service.

Freewheeling

154. **The 'Rover' Safety Bicycle** was invented in 1886. It established the template for the diamond-framed, chain-driven bicycles that we know today. W F Keen and Alfred Gladden were two of the first cycle dealers in Chesham.

155. **Early experiments.** Before the Safety Bicycle, several ideas had been tried, including the 'Boneshaker' (1867) and the 'Penny Farthing' (1869). These dangerous machines were generally limited to use by adventurous young men. The risk-averse preferred tricycles, such as this one photographed locally. Queen Victoria owned a similar one, but it is unlikely that she ever rode it!

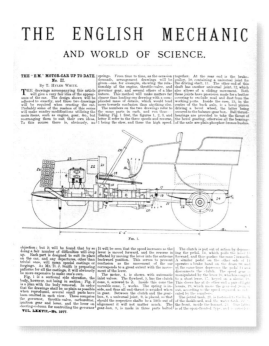

156 and 157. **The Cheeld story.** The women of the Cheeld family demonstrate Chesham's first motor car *(above, right)*. The bicycle had become a symbol of female emancipation, but men were drawn to the petrol engine. Mr Sidney Cheeld, an engineer, built this car at Lord's Mill, completing it in 1904. He used a design from a series of construction articles in the weekly magazine 'The English Mechanic and World of Science'. He called the E.M. motor car 'Emma'. It had two cyclinders and 8 horse power. Mr Cheeld's grandson is currently the blacksmith at Hawridge.

158. **'Emma',** Chesham's first motor car, still does the London to Brighton Veteran Car Run. Fittingly, it was a woman, Joan Shawe, who restored the car over the years 1954 to 1972. It is now owned by Mrs Shawe's son John, in Hertfordshire. The family has taken part in the London to Brighton event over 30 times.

159. **The Cestreham Cycling & Athletics Club** was founded in 1887. Locally-made cycles were the 'Cestreham', 'Albatross' and 'Reliance'. From these early roadster machines developed the lightweight racing bikes of the 1930s, touring bikes of the 1950s, small-wheeled shoppers of the '60s, BMX in the '70s and mountain bikes in the 1980s. Cycling remains today as popular as ever.

"As youngsters we were rarely without our bikes, which gave us a wonderful freedom to roam far and wide. Les Stronnell was a popular character and was a great source of help in maintaining our steeds. Most youngsters did not acquire a new bike until well into their teens, having to make do with second-hand ones or family hand-me-downs. Consequently, Les was much in demand for recovering spare parts to keep these ageing machines in roadworthy condition. His workshop was always a cosy haven in cold weather and one could generally be sure of a cup of tea there as well."

Bill Howard in 2016, *remembering the cycle shop still run by Les's son.*

(With thanks to cycle history research by Anne Crabbe).

160. **A very early Scott motorcycle** and ornate wicker sidecar, about 1911, on one of the roads leading into Chesham

161. **Arthur and Rose Smith, Higham Road,** probably late 1930s. The motorcycle is a Panther, made by the Yorkshire-based firm Phelon & Moore prior to the decline of the British motorcycle industry after WWII. Various members of the Smith family lived at 23 Higham Road for most of the 20th century.

162. **A 1960-model Vespa scooter,** as sold by Mayo & Hawkes, est.1928, *(off-camera, left)*. Perhaps Mr Beck – with no socks, no helmet, beard and pipe – is heading for the Embassy Cinema in Germain Street! From 1961, learner riders were restricted to machines of no more than 250cc capacity in order to deal with the high number of motorcycling fatalities. In 1973, safety helmets were made compulsory for moped and motorcycle riders and the top speed for mopeds was set at 30mph. A new accompanied motorcycle test was introduced in 1989, prompted by a continuation of alarmingly high accident figures.

The Motor Age

163. **The story of the motor car** in our town has already been told in a previously published book 'Chesham in Living Memory'. Early vehicles such as this one *(far left)*, pictured in Broad Street in the early 1900s, were quickly superceded by faster and more comfortable models.

164. **This Austin Clifton Heavy Twelve-Four of 1926** was seen regularly around town during the 1960s. It was owned by Hungarian illustrator Val Biro, who lived at Fullers Hill, and it was the subject of his very successful 'Gumdrop' children's books. Gumdrop was regularly serviced at the Wey Lane Garage, and often seen in Stanley Avenue at the family home of Alan Fry, another Hungarian, and the father of the well-known comedian Stephen Fry. Traditionalists such as Val Biro could do nothing to check the advancing technology of the motor car.

165. **W Foster's garage** in the High Street supplied charabancs during the 1920s for seaside and sporting outings *(see p52)*. It closed a decade before the explosive rise in petrol prices of 1973 which failed to end the unbridled enthusiasm of motorists.

166. **1960s' cars** were arguably the most stylish vehicles ever built, but they were poor on driver safety, and were potential death traps. New cars are loaded with safety equipment that we now take for granted: crumple zones, airbags, headrests and safety glass for example.

167. **The expansion of petrol stations and motor garages** in the 20th century mirrored the rapid demise of the old blacksmiths and shoeing forges, as cars replaced horses as the popular mode of transport. This is the Plough Filling Station at the foot of White Hill in the early 1960s.

"We know what happens to people who stay in the middle of the road. They get run down."

"I read the newspapers avidly. It is my one form of continuous fiction."

Famous quotes from Aneurin (Nye) Bevan. He was the Labour Minister responsible for the establishment of the NHS. His wife was Jennie Lee, also a Minister in the same Government

and a prime mover in the creation of the Open University. They came to live at Wood Farm, Asheridge, near Chesham during the 1950s.

"Miss Jennie Lee's Accident in Blucher Street, Chesham:

Readers will remember that Miss Lee (Mrs Aneurin Bevan) knocked down and injured one of three passing pedestrians."
The Bucks Examiner, April 1955

168. and 169. **A 1950s' Triumph Mayflower and a Standard 10** in a very quiet looking Broad Street and Broadway. In 1930 there were about two million motor vehicles in Britain, with 7,000 people killed in road accidents each year. Today there are well over ten times that many vehicles, yet only half the number of road deaths. Zebra crossings were introduced in 1951 and, in 1968, the Highway Code introduced updated illustrations of road signs with the new 'continental' design. The Green Cross Code was launched in 1978.

170. **Milton Road,** 1964. Housing estates were built beyond the Chesham valley bottom from the 1920s onwards, and the rise of the motor car allowed people to drive down to the town's amenities, and back home up the steep hills.

171. Buying horses for the First World War, Chesham Broadway, 4th August 1914. Of the one million horses sent from Britain overseas to help with the war effort, only 62,000 returned home. This was the forgotten tragedy of the Great War that recently regained the public's attention. Local resident Diana Shorey recounts that her grandfather Henry Darvell, a farmer of Waterside, was upset at being forced to lose seven of his horses to the army.

What did return from the war were thousands of lorry chassis that were made redundant after hostilities. These were put to use for charabancs and buses, and formed the basis of the new local bus service.

172. **Open top charabancs** were popular in the 1920s, such as this one from Foster's Garage. They were used for pleasure trips, for example to Windsor for a walk by the Thames, and seated about 28 people. With an average speed of 12mph, much of the day was spent on the road.

173. **Amersham & District Motor Bus Company Ltd.** There were several privately owned bus firms, but by far the largest between 1919 and 1933 was Amersham & District, which operated from The Griffin in Old Amersham. (See Neil Lamond & John Hutchinson's 2017 book 'The Pride of Bucks').

174. **Chesham Broadway** was the town's first car park until Star Yard was opened up in 1938. It remains to be the focus of Chesham's bus transport, as well as giving access to the town's railway via Station Road, constructed in 1889, and the current site of the taxi rank.

176. **London Transport's** 336 to Watford outside Godwin's Snack Bar in the 1950s.

175. **London Transport** took over local bus operations from 1933 with its 'Green Line' service. Many people came out from London by bus to enjoy the Chiltern countryside. Local bus usage peaked in the 1950s prior to the great rise in private car ownership, the popularity of television, and the availability of a local taxi service. After the break up of central control in 1986, buses came in all colours and were often branded with advertising and run by smaller local operators under contract to Transport for Buckinghamshire.

(See Keith Fletcher's Monograph on local buses & coaches available at Chesham Reference Library).

177. **London Transport's** 372 to Ley Hill outside Broadway Newsagents. The Chiltern Link branding dates this scene to the 1980s.

"On 9th December 1938 the death of Mrs Ford was reported in 'The Bucks Examiner'. Bus drivers and conductors at the Amersham Garage were saddened with this news. Mrs Ford had always invited them in when they arrived at their turnaround point of Ley Hill. She kept the kettle on the hob and they could warm their hands and feet whether it was 8 o'clock in the morning or 10.30 at night."

Keith Fletcher, local historian, on how buses lacked heating until 1962

178. **Rover Bus & Coach Service** was run by Jesse Dell of Lycrome Road from 1928. Here is one of his coaches outside the Cum-U-In café, arriving from Hemel Hempstead.

179. and 180. **Taxis.** Sam Rance *(above)* waits for customers at the Chesham Station taxi rank. He worked for Ron & Barbara Gilbert, who ran Radio Cars from 1956. It was Ron's father, Percy Gilbert, who had set up the town's first taxi firm in 1948. The Ford Consul was a favoured car of the early '60s. A third generation member of the family, Chris Gilbert, continues Gilbert's Taxis to this day.

Chapter Seven
Shopping

Milk from Farm to Fridge

181. **Joseph How delivering milk to Hivings Hill, 1920s.** In an era when a lack of refrigeration meant milk would quickly spoil, it was delivered straight from the farm to houses daily. Daisy Hunt, née Puddephatt, remembered how milkmen would measure the milk out in gills from large churns on the back of the cart – four gills in one pint – poured straight into the household's jugs. The only milk they could buy from a shop was condensed in a tin and very sweet.

182. **Milkmen** delivered to almost all Chesham households by electric milk float during the 1960s and '70s. Having your milk brought to your door was the only easy way of getting a daily 'pinta'. Foil tops were preceded by ones made from cardboard. Chesham Dairies had been established in 1947 by several independent milkmen, and was sold to Brazier's in 1980. In that year, nine tenths of all milk consumed in town still arrived via a glass bottle on the doorstep during the early hours. Widespread refrigeration and expanding supermarkets mean that milkmen have now become only a premium service. About ten percent of homes still use a milkman, but the number continues to fall.

183. **Supermarket milk.** These days, milk is stored at a farm for anything up to two days in a refrigerated tank. It is then collected by tanker and taken to a processing plant, which could be up to 150 miles away, where it is stored for no more than four days. The milk is pasteurised by rapid heating and cooling which kills off both good and bad bacteria, but markedly increases shelf life. It is separated and standardised by removing all the butterfat cream and then adding a certain percentage back to make 'whole milk', 'semi-skimmed' or 'skimmed'. It is homogenised by breaking the fat into tiny particles until it is unable to rise to the top – this is why you don't get the line of cream on top of your milk any more. Milk is packed in plastic cartons and trucked all over the country, to shops and wholesalers. By the time the milk ends up in your fridge, it could be anything up to two weeks old!

184. **Milk is now coming direct to the door again**, along with our bulk shopping. In the mid-1990s, Tesco started exploring the potential of the new internet technology. They could use their existing superstores for collecting online grocery shopping orders and were the first big company to launch an online service in 1996. Currently, Sainsbury's and Waitrose (Ocado) are often seen delivering locally alongside Tesco. However, the milk now carried to your door with your online shopping has had a long and complicated journey from the farm.

From Residential to Commercial

Up until the 19th century, Church Street was the main area of commercial activity in town, and the High Street was primarily residential, having originally followed the path of the river upstream from Market Square. The Broadway, otherwise known as Pillory Green, was the traditional gathering place for fairs, ceremonies, punishments and celebrations.

Very old photographs show how townsfolk began to sell goods from their front rooms or parlours in and around the Broadway. Slowly the centre of commerce shifted into the new town centre.

185. **A toy shop, c.1890** has attracted a gathering of children. Note the locally-made wooden hoops outside.

186. **The old toy shop stood on the site of No.63 The Broadway,** High Street, which currently houses Biedronka Polish Delicatessen.

187. **Catling's Provision Stores,** pictured at the foot of the page, occupied the site at the beginning of the 20th centry, but note that the premises was rebuilt once again during the intervening period.

The High Street has a broad range of architecture dating from several centuries, reflecting this constant change of use. Some beautiful old buildings have been preserved, and others – such as the gabled Coffee Tavern next door to No.63 – have been unsympathetically modernised.

The location of No. 63 The Broadway.

The House of Tree

188. **The House of Tree** was an outfitters, drapers and shop dealing in haberdashery and fashions, in two attractive buildings demolished to make way for the original Waitrose supermarket in the High Street.

189. **The International Stores,** was a leading chain of grocers, swallowed up by the supermarkets in 1972 after almost 100 years of trading. This branch was at the foot of Station Road.

"LITTLE HOPE NOW FOR THE HOUSE OF TREE: Chesham housewives seem decidedly against the proposals. In a random survey in Chesham High Street, four out of five shoppers were against a third supermarket. Mr C J Spencer, manager of the International Stores, was quite adamant. 'The town is adequately served by supermarkets already and this third one will mean a smaller share of the cake for everyone.' Mr Stanley Cox, Chesham historian, thought otherwise. 'Fetch it down,' he said 'the building is of no interest as far as I am concerned'." *Bucks Examiner 1967*

Many residents remember the terribly tragic day in January 1971 when a 16-year-old girl was shot and killed in this store by a boy who was one year older. He claimed to be in love with her, but his advances had been rebuffed. He was sentenced to life imprisonment.

190. **The ultra-modern Waitrose building** was the third supermarket in town, following Tesco and Stitchers. Its brutalist design was, and remains to be, highly controversial.

'Corner' Shops

191. **No.74 Broad Street,** where, at the turn of the century, Mr White advertised tickets for the Great Central Railway, which ran from Manchester to London, with links to the Metropolitan Line.

192. **Bone's Newsagents & Tobacconists, 241 Berkhampstead Road,** photographed at Christmas 1906, shortly after Alfred Bone opened the shop. He was a well-known football player for the Chesham Generals. His son George took over the business in 1958.

193. **Nora Hendy outside Brackley's at No.74,** where she and her husband had a share of the business when Mr Brackley retired. Tobacco advertising predominates.

> "We used to buy our fireworks from Bone's.
> No controls then on errant youngsters and we delighted in tormenting the girls with casually lobbed Brocks Bangers or the totally unpredictable ballistic qualities of the Standard Jumping Betty! These days it would attract a costly, time-consuming but totally ineffectual ASBO. Then it was a summarily administered clip round the ear if you were foolish enough to be collared by an observant adult."
>
> *William (Bill) Howard, born 1939*

194. **In 2017** the premises is still known as Brackley's under the banner of Costcutter. Lottery tickets are shown as available seven days a week.

195. **Plested's, Waterside,** photographed about 1999 by the author in the sure knowledge that it was one of the last of its kind in Chesham.

No.7 Market Square

196. Print & paper spanning three centuries at the same premises

"In 1936 Harold and Nip Blundell first visited the pretty town of Chesham, nestling in the Chiltern Hills, whilst Harold was playing against Chesham United. As luck would have it, the couple spotted an advertisement for the sale of a newsagent/bookshop in the Market Square. Scraping together their savings and pooling them with Harold's brother Eddie's, they managed to buy the shop. The two young couples, Nip and Harold, Eddie and his wife, Mary, lived on the two floors above the shop. Thanks to Eddie's extra income as a skilled carpenter they balanced the books and managed to draw wages of £1.00 for each couple!

Thankfully, the bookshop thrived and gradually built a fine reputation as a source of quality reading matter as well as a newsagents and stationers. Harold, a popular local figure, helped found the Rotary Club of Chesham together with other local businessmen. He went on to become President in 1958.

Such was Harold's dedication to the business and his customers that when the harsh winter of 1963 prevented him from driving down Eskdale Avenue at 5.00am to collect the papers from the station, he took to tobogganing down White Hill to collect them instead! The business continued to thrive throughout the fifties and sixties. The Blundells looked at buying other shops in nearby towns but decided that they were content with running one multi-faceted business.

Harold had always promised himself that he would retire at 58 years old. This he nearly did, selling the shop in 1965. However, he retained the printing works, at the rear of the premises, and had it virtually doubled in size to enable him to continue printing letterheads, posters, cheque books and pamphlets." *Peter Blundell*

197. **Smith Brothers' Stationers & Booksellers** *(below, right)* were carrying out the same line of business at No.7 in 1894 as is currently offered. The building goes back well before that though, to about 1620, and at one time was a pub called the Bull & Butcher. Around 1856 it was Thomas Jordan's shop. He made grandfather clocks and also installed the clock in the Market Hall, seen here at midday.

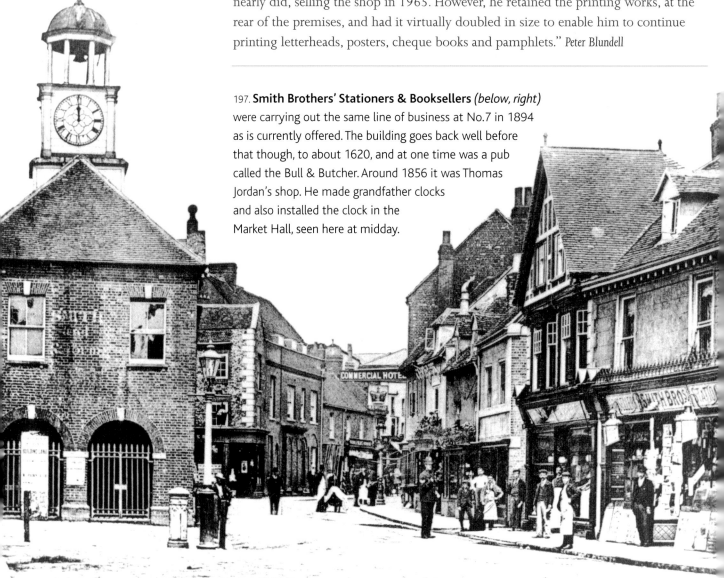

198. **Blundell's Bookshop** in the early 1960s. Over 50 years later it is still being renovated with care!

199. **Hazeltine's** supplied these 'crested china' replicas of the town's war memorial, which was unveiled in 1921. The Hazeltine family ran the stationery & newsagency business from No.7 some time between 1924 and 1936.

200. **Chiltern Office Efficiency** was re-located to No.7 in 1976 by David Rowley, in partnership with Graham Woodward, sales director, seen here in the shop.

"MARKET SQUARE GET A NEW SHOP: Until a month ago one of the oldest and best preserved shops was just an ordinary newsagents and stationers. Now the Town Bookshop, formerly Blundell's, opens its doors as the modern shop to cater for all tastes in books, stationery, periodicals and newspapers. With the workmen now adding the finishing touches the transformation is complete. The regular delivery of newspapers each morning to between 400 and 450 people in Chesham will continue. As an extra attraction, Mr Daniels hopes to feature local authors' books when they are published."
'*The Bucks Examiner*', *late 1960s.*

201. **JPS Stationers.** In 1995, a commercial office supplies business expanded out of the Thames Valley to serve the Chilterns from No.7, with Ray Williams acting as shop manager. In 2011, Ray took over to form a traditional family business with wife Heather and son Steve. .

A High Street for Pedestrians

Of the town's butchers, we have lost Gomm's, Derrick's and Eric's to St Mary's Way, but still have Gerry Martins' in the pedestrianised High Street. As for bakers, we have Darvell's, which has traded since 1838. We even have a candlestick maker up on Hivings Hill!

202. **The High Street,** looking south from Station Road towards the Market Square at the turn of the century. Note the mix of shops and residential premises.

203. and 204. **The pedestrianised High Street.** There is a wonderful similarity between the scene at the top of the page and the state of the current High Street. The photograph of Lagoon (ladies fashion), Mirage (menswear) and Iceland supermarket dates from about 1992, two years after pedestrianisation and soon after the construction of the clock tower. Since through-traffic was banned, it is a much healthier environment in which people can walk, especially the elderly, and parents with young children. The George & Dragon photo dates from 2000.

205. **Traffic congestion, 1967.** St Mary's Way relief road and East Street service road took the bulk of motorised transport out of the town centre. Many shopkeepers felt that this move damaged their trade, but the author strongly believes that it was the only viable option for modern traffic levels combined with the narrow High Street. The Chesham Society is currently promoting plans to build a new shopping centre over Star Yard car park, thus giving potential through-traffic a clearer indication of a town worth visiting beyond the walls of St Mary's Way.

Find out more in the book 'Chesham in Living Memory – The Age of the Motor Car'.

206. to 208. **Unfamiliar walkways.** These three images from the early 1960s show parts of Church Street and Parsonage Lane, now obliterated by the construction of St Mary's Way in 1968, and the entrance to Stratford's Yard which was completely demolished to make way for East Street in 1966.

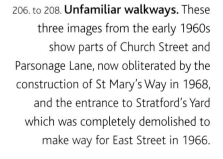

Chapter Eight
Services

The Police

210. and 211. **The second Police Station** in Broad Street, pictured here in 1987, the year of its closure. The old cell block is pictured before the building was converted to offices, known as Copsham House, and then to flats.

209. **In 1861, this Police Station was built on open fields in Broad Street.** Previously the town's lockup and gaol was in Amy Lane – a brick-and-flint cottage which still stands and has bars at the cellar windows. Criminals were held for up to seven days, before being moved on to Aylesbury Gaol. Chesham's industrial Newtown grew up around this Victorian building, which served Chesham's police force until the 1930s.

"My three-greats-grandfather, Matthew Darvell, was found guilty in 1812 of stealing a sack of flour from his employer Thomas Wright of Amen Mill (later Amy Mill). He was sentenced to seven years' transportation. However, the people of Chesham got up a petition to save him. In all, 72 people including his employer Thomas Wright signed the petition. As a result, Matthew was shown mercy and served a short time in Aylesbury gaol.

Matthew turns up again in 1830 during the Swing Riots [*when rural workers of the arable Home Counties rose up, demanding higher wages and an end to the threshing machines which destroyed their employment*]. He was arrested in Chesham carrying an axe over his shoulder, using threatening language and offering his services to any mob that might require them. He spent another six months in gaol.

He married three times and died in 1860, aged 89. On his death certificate it shows the cause of death as senility, gangrene and general decay."

Roberta Crosby, Wiltshire

(For more on the Swing Riots see the book 'Buckinghamshire Machine Breakers' by Jill Chambers)

212. **The third Police Station** in Broad Street opened in 1988 and is set for closure by 2019.

The Fire Brigade

213. **A volunteer fire brigade** was set up in Chesham in 1846 and this horse-drawn manual hand pump was being used in 1889. Note the heavy beards which must have created a fire hazard!

214. **Posed outside the Bury in 1913,** the Fire Brigade, overseen by Chesham Urban District Council, had acquired a steam fire engine, an escape ladder and canvas hoses.

216. **At the gallop.** Back in the days when, in the event of a fire, the volunteer brigade had to be rounded up from local factories, and the horses gathered and harnessed, then the steam-boiler lit and heated up, it's a wonder that the Fire Brigade was able to have any effect on local blazes at all.

215. **A Leyland motorised engine,** purchased in 1923, was named 'Norah' after Brigade Captain Ralph Howard's daughter.

217. **The old upper High Street fire station** and bell tower, used from 1938 until the end of WWII, after which it became an ambulance station. It was demolished in 1980.

218. **A Bedford fire engine**, Bellingdon Road, early 1960s.

219. **A Commer fire engine,** Bellingdon Road, 1970s.

"What I didn't know was that the fire alarm had gone off and because I was deaf I had not heard it. Luckily for me, Edie realised I was not there and came running back shouting for me to 'come quick, the factory is on fire'. Indeed it was, we all stood outside and watched it burning. If it had not been for Edie missing me I might not be here to tell the tale." *Hilda Jane Brown, née Birch, who worked with Edith Channer at Beechwoods brush factory.*

222. **Beechwood's brush factory fire,** March 1930.

220. **A reconstruction of the 1913 photograph** *(pic 214)* made by the brigade in the 1990s, at the same Bury location.

221. **Demolition of the Bellingdon Road fire station** with a crew from 1993. George Wilkinson, retired station commander, then aged 83, and of Gladstone Road, wears an old brass helmet.

223. **Fire above Bennett's hardware store,** High Street, 1970s.

224. **Gas explosion** at Scamps Wine Bar, High Street, 1988.

225. **Bellingdon Road Fire Station,** was built about 1946 and is pictured here in 1990 with GMC and Dodge vehicles. It was demolished three years later.

226. **The current Fire Station with its drill tower** was opened in 1994 by Baroness Blatch.

The Cottage Hospital

227. **Chesham Cottage Hospital** was established in 1869 by public subscription, with just seven beds. Before that, people who were ill would have visited an apothecary, voluntary hospital, surgeon or, at worst, the Workhouse Infirmary. There were no ambulances then, just a 'fly', or fast horse & carriage.

228. **Doctors Long & Churchill** with nurses in 1890. Dr Churchill (with hat and beard) had survived the typhoid fever outbreak in Chesham of 1871. His colleague Dr Faithorn and three nurses died. An Iron Hospital was constructed alongside the Cottage Hospital for patients with infectious diseases – and later moved to the Vale.

"I caught diphtheria in 1940 as a child and was taken to the isolation hospital. While there I picked up scarlet fever and was in for three months. When I got home I had quite a few ailments and ended up having my tonsils and adenoids removed at Chesham Hospital. All I remember is fighting like a tiger when they tried to put the mask over my face. No pre-meds in those days. I came round with a dreadful sore throat and was given ice-cream, which was most soothing. I was lucky, as many others died."

Margaret Johnson (nee Herrington)

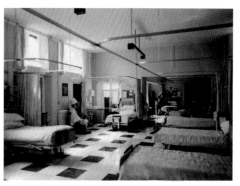

229. to 232. **Enlarged in 1923/4,** the premises also gained a portable X-ray machine, purchased from Germany. Taken over by the NHS in 1948, the hospital continued until 2005, when the town was promised a new Healthzone *(see page 26)*. The Cottage Hospital had looked after older people and offered respite care, but now local people must go to Amersham Hospital. Locals were also disappointed that there was to be no X-ray department, in-patient beds or physiotherapy – simply doctors' surgeries and a pharmacy.

Media & Advertising

234. 'The Chesham Advertiser' *(below)* was one of a number of short-lived broadsheet newspapers printed in the 19th century. The author has two copies from the launch year of 1892 that have survived in very good condition.

233. 'The Chesham Companion to the Almanacks' was begun in 1844 by the printer and stationer William Hepburn, and sold for 3d. This 1847 edition features an advertisement for Arthur Liberty, draper of Chesham. He was the father of Sir Arthur Lasenby Liberty, founder of Liberty & Co., of London.

235. 'The Chesham Examiner' *(top)* was founded in 1889 and much later became known as 'The Bucks Examiner'. This torn copy in the author's possession dates from 1894. The title still exists as 'The Buckinghamshire Examiner', and although its current masthead claims a start date of 1853, this does in fact mark the beginning of William Broadwater's 'Buckinghamshire Advertiser,' the sister title now also owned by Trinity Mirror. Whilst the offices of 'The Bucks Examiner' were in Germain Street, Chesham, it was very popular with the townspeople. Long may it continue.

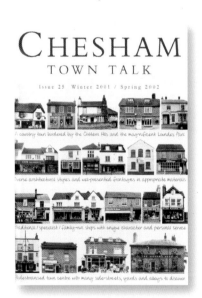

236. 'Chesham Town Talk' began as a community newsletter in 1994 and developed into a high quality, not-for-profit magazine run by a large volunteer team. As such, it lasted for 20 years and provided a positive perspective on the town, in contrast to the 'bad news sells' approach of the general media.

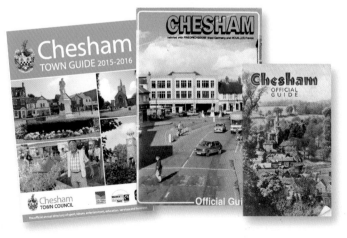

237. 'The Chesham Town Guide' has been issued since at least 1947 as the official guide to the town's council activities, businesses, sports clubs, civic societies and entertainment venues. Also, in the early 20th century, Pigot's and Kelly's Directories were an early equivalent of the BT Yellow Pages.

238. 'Your Chesham' is the latest addition to Chesham's news scene, established in 2010.

Communications

"When Charles I opened up his 'royal mail' for use by the public in 1635, he laid the foundations for the Post Office as an institution. Oliver Cromwell established the General Post Office in 1657. The beginning of uniform penny postage in 1840 made sending mail affordable to all for the first time."
Keith Fletcher, local historian, 2011.

239. and 240. Letters from Chesham.
The first is dated 27th February 1800 and has a curved style Chesham postmark. It cost thirteen times as much to send as the second letter, dated 15th December 1840, which has the famous one penny postage stamp known as the 'penny black', introduced that year.

241. The Parcels Post Cart.
Chesham's Post Office has had many locations, but in 1845 the Postmaster was George Devereux, and in 1890 his daughter Marion had taken over as Postmistress from this premises at No.7 Market Square (see page 58). In 1892, letters for hand delivery between Amersham and Berkhamsted – via Chesham – were carried by 'Old Joe' who tramped the double journey daily.

242. and 243. Telecommunications.
In 1870 (prior to this photograph), the Post Office took control of the telegraph system and in 1906 it added the telephone service to its operations. The telegraph was the first source of electronic communication, but the telephone was favoured as it could be used from home. Before this, the time it took for news to travel from one place to another could be many days. In 1964, an automated telephone exchange had to be built behind the Post Office to cope with the 560,000 calls a year within Chesham.

(Acknowledgement in full to a Monograph: 'The History of the Post Office in Chesham' written by Keith Fletcher, 2011).

244. and 245. **Chesham Post Office** was based at 77 High Street from 1903 until 1991, and returned between 2010 and 2015 to this tall 17th century building.

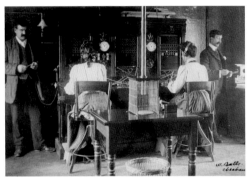

246. and 247. **The Post Office counter, 1912 and Chesham's first telephone exchange.** There were only 60 telephone lines in Chesham in 1906, and by 1958 there was a capacity for just 600 lines. Telephone ownership took off in the 1960s.

248. **'What ho old sport!'** Postcards from 1906 to 1957, with stamps depicting the reigns of three monarchs. Missing is King Edward VIII, who abdicated after less than a year on the throne in 1936.

249. **Replacement of red phone boxes,** The Broadway, 1988.

250. **Current postal services.** Despite the advent of emails, the internet and text messages, we still rely heavily on the Post Office and Royal Mail. Following the closure of many sub-Post Offices, the central premises currently run by Jit Mistry is busier than ever and the Howard Road sorting office, opened in 1988, is a hub of activity. Mark Cundy has delivered Chesham High Street's mail since 2000.

Chapter Nine
Leisure Time

Cultural Connections

251/2. **Few great names of literature** have emanated from Chesham, although D H Lawrence lived in Bellingdon for a short time. Just after his marriage to Frieda Weekly, née von Richthofen, in 1914 and when he was writing *The Rainbow*, he resided at Bellingdon Farm Cottages, Hawridge Lane *(right)*. They formed an intellectual nucleus with other writer friends, such as Katherine Mansfield and John Middleton Murry. Gilbert Cannan lived with his wife in The Windmill at Cholesbury and there the Lawrences met Compton Mackenzie, the artist Mark Gertler and the historian G M Trevelyan. But by 1915 the Lawrences were disenchanted with life in the Chilterns and had moved away!

(c/o research by Anne Crabbe)

253/4/5. **Chesham Musical Theatre Company** is the town's oldest established theatrical group, having started in 1922 and migrating over the decades through many name changes and venues. In 1928 *(left)* they performed *Iolanthe* as the Cestreham Singers & Players, starring Dorothy Hanks, Edwin Blake, Thomas Stillman, Florence Woodard and Harold Green. The venue was the Town Hall in Market Square. In 1951 they performed *The Gondoliers* as the Chesham Amateur Operatic Society at the Embassy Cinema. From 1976 shows were put on at the original Elgiva Theatre, which was rebuilt in 1998 on the opposite side of St Mary's Way *(left)*.

256. **The Little Theatre by the Park** is Chesham's alternative theatre venue and in 2016 a new group, Voice of the Show, performed with Guy Siner *(right)*, star of TV's *'Allo 'Allo!*, who lives in the town.

(For the history of Chesham's theatre clubs see Geoff Hale's book 'Entertaining Chesham'.)

Cinema

THE EMBASSY CINEMA: "We queued for an hour to watch 'Mary Poppins'; the queue went right round the corner and into the car park. I loved Saturday morning pictures, especially sitting at the top in the front and watching the naughty boys dropping stuff on the kids below." *Angie Delaney*

THE WHITE OWL CAFÉ: "I used the White Owl in the late '60s. It was the place to be in Chesham – pinball machine and jukebox – what more did you want in those days?" *Roger Shirley*

DOLLING'S SWEET SHOP: "Sweets before Saturday morning pictures at the Embassy. All the sweets were in big jars and you bought a quarter of sweets in a paper bag. Rhubarb & Custards were my favourite!" *Ann Barwell*

257. **Cinema going grew dramatically in the 1930s** with the advent of sound and then colour films. The Embassy Cinema in Germain Street was opened in 1937 by the film actor, John Loder. Designed by David Nye in opulent art deco style, it had an entrance surrounded by neon lights, which opened on to a spacious foyer, and sweeping stairs led to a stylish chrome and glass café. After the war, attendances at the Embassy boomed, so much so that the old Astoria cinema in the Broadway closed in 1959. However, the later impact of television and video meant that it was sold to the EMI chain in 1975 and, despite substantial refurbishment, it closed in 1983. The Townbridge Court retirement housing now occupies the site.

258. **Demolition of The Embassy Cinema**, 1983. If The Embassy had survived a little longer, it might well have been the subject of a remarkable rescue such as that of The Rex in Berkhamsted.

259. and 260. **The White Owl café and Dolling's sweet shop** were popular with cinema-goers. The Embassy had its own café and restaurant run by Nancy Haslehurst and Ernst Schwerzmann. They went on to start Alpine Caterers, which lasted for around 35 years and they created a purpose-built kitchen in Higham Road, which is currently used by Seasons Catering.

Lowndes Park

261. **Bury Hill House.** Once the upper parsonage of the rectorial manor of Chesham Leicester, this large house was built in Elizabethan times and demolished by the Lowndes family at the start of the 19th century. It was the home of the Ashfields, Whichcotes and Skottowes, the latter giving their name to the pond which originally formed part of their pleasure gardens. An avenue of elms was planted in 1760, then felled and replanted in 1845. It was felled again in 1950 and has sadly never been reinstated. In 1953 the Lowndes family gave the Park to the people of Chesham. The avenue is now known as Rue de Houilles, after the French twin town.

262. **The avenue of elm trees** in Bury Hill Walk was one of the finest in England.

263. **Felling of the elms,** by the local engineering firm T T Boughton in 1950. They used a steam-driven 'Foden' timber tractor for haulage. The avenue was never properly replaced.

264. **Winter skating** on Skottowe's Pond in the 1930s was charged at 2d; free on Sundays. When the pond froze over in the 1970s, the local children were once again seen playing on the ice, but these days the winters are rarely cold enough for a heavy freeze, and health & safety executives would frown on such an activity!

265. **Rowing on Skottowe's Pond** with Catling's Farm (demolished in 1959) in the background. Cows from the farm used to graze around the pond, before the lower park was leased by the Council for public use in the 1920s. In the 1930s there were three boats which could be hired from Reginald Gray, the park keeper, for 9d for half-an-hour. Boys tended to row as far from the attendant as possible to gain extra minutes! Note the pollarded elms along the Avenue.

266. **A glimpse of the paddling pool** built in the 1950s; demolished in the 1990s.

267. **Lowndes Park playground,** 1956. Janet and Ann Cottington swinging on the 'witch's hat' roundabout. This play equipment was later outlawed by health & safety directives!

268. **Construction of the fountain on the bandstand,** 1971, by Brian & Cyril Freeman on behalf of Harman's Builders.

269. **The fountain completed.** Geoffrey Arnold and John Motture, students at the Technical College, enjoy the new Park feature!

270. **BMX and skate boarding ramps** have been a feature of the Park's facilities since the 1980s.

271. **Bands in the Park** is an event held on summer days on the levelled bandstand, which now has a contemporary canopy and labyrinth design.

The Sports Pages

Bowls

272. to 275. **Chesham Bowling Club**. Bowls has been played in Chesham since the early 1900s, originally on Mr G Darvell's lawn at Treacher's Orchard, off Bellingdon Road. In 1912 a formal Club was established and the following year an area of land in Lowndes Park was leased from the Squire to be converted to a bowling green. This was the only flat part of the Park, known as 'The Level' and was in fact the site of the Skottowe family's Bury Hill House, which was demolished by the Lowndes family *(see page 70)*. Pictured left is Dick Goodson who, in 1936, won the English Bowling Association singles championship trophy, and went on the win international honours.

(See the book 'Chesham Bowling Club: 1912 – 2012')

276. to 278. **Chess Vale Bowling Club** was established in 1931 at the rear of 31 High Street on behalf of the Chesham Conservative Club. This green was later isolated between the McMinn Centre and East Street. Subsidence eventually meant its removal to Asheridge Road in 2004. Pictured are Tom Cottington and Mr T Bignall with Championship cups from 1960 and 1961.

(Broadway Bowling Club, based at the foot of Lowndes Avenue and currently relocating, is another group of Chesham bowling enthusiasts).

Golf

279. First tee. After playing at Hill Farm, these six well-to-do golfers obtained permission from Lord Chesham to play on Ley Hill Common. The 9-hole Chesham Golf Club was instituted there in 1900.

280. This 18-hole golf course at Chartridge Park was established in 1989 by Bill Wells and Peter Gibbins.

(See: 'Chesham & Ley Hill Golf Club, the First 100 Years,' published in the year 2000).

Cricket

281. to 283. W G Grace, that most famous of cricketers, *(the bearded gentleman seated centre)*, was invited by Squire William Lowndes to bring a team down to the Meadow in the years 1905 through 1908. Cricket had been played in town since the early 19th century *(see p17)*. The golden era of Chesham Cricket Club was from the 1950s into the early 1970s *(the sepia photo is of Geoff Reynolds calling the toss in 1958, whilst playing for Bucks versus Kent, in front of an old wooden pavilion*. In 1963 Fred Truman opened a new building, which sadly burnt down in a recent arson attack. In line with the decline and ascendency of the Club, a brand new pavilion has now been built and in 2016 the team *(pictured)* won the Thames Valley League. (Coming soon: A history of the Club by Peter Gibbins & Rod Dowle.)

Rugby

284/5. Chesham Rugby Club, nicknamed 'The Stags' was set up in 1982 in a town dominated by football. They moved from Marston field, to the Moor and on to Chesham Park Community College. Now that the school has been converted to an Academy, the Club is building a clubhouse on site for 2018.

The Rugby Club has teams for men, women, juniors and minis. Photographs from all these sections featured in a 2015 World Cup advertising campaign by JC Decaux that was seen nationwide, including at Heathrow Airport, railway stations up and down the country, shopping centres and roadside billboards.

Swimming

(See 'A Brief History of the Open-Air Swimming Pool' by Garry Marshall, 1997).

286. **'The bathing nuisance'.** In 1898 the Council agreed to put a corrugated iron fence between a well-used pool of the River Chess and the houses of Shantung Place, off to the right-hand side of this scene. Not until 1912 was a formal swimming pool and associated buildings constructed.

287. **Harry Podbury** of Chesham gives us an idea of what the original pool in the river looked like.

288. **Austere changing facilities** for Whitehill School pupils, 1930s.

289. **An altogether more leisurely environment,** 2001.

290. **Reconstruction,** 1964, in a modern style typical of the era.

291. **Redevelopment** took place in 1997, with pitched roofing.

"I learned to swim in the Town Pool, which was then fed directly from a spring – and was deathly cold! It was just a corrugated iron enclosure with a few cubicles, more or less in the same place as the present pool." *Richard Prior – a 1930s' childhood*

"The fair would come to the Moor probably twice a year and, on one occasion, a circus. We arrived at the Pool one morning to find the circus people had broken in and washed their horses down in the water. But we still went in!"
Pam Bayliss (nee Sale-Thorn) – a 1940s' childhood

Football

292. and 293. **Then & Now:** *(far left)* a Chesham player in the Berks & Bucks FA League, 1900-02. The amalgamation of Chesham Town and Chesham Generals in 1919 consolidated senior football 40 years after it was first established in the town; *(left)* Chesham United beating Kings Langley 1–0 at the Meadow, 28th August 2017.

294. **Opening of the new ground** at The Meadow, 31st October 1931. Arch & Edie Hawkes are seated far right, half way back, about to watch Lord Chesham lead the players on to the pitch. This stand burnt down in 1983, but the Club survived that troubled decade.

295. **George Terpilowski** of Chesham United collects the Berks & Bucks Cup in 1948, having beaten Wycombe Wanderers 2-1. The following year the Club had its worst ever defeat: 12-1 to Grays! United's history mixes success and failure in equal measure.

296. **Chesham United at Wembley.** The crowds advance on the stadium, Saturday 20th April, 1968, photographed by Donald Dixon. *(Pamela Seymour in the red coat, Leigh and Paul Dixon as young lads, Charlie Dunkerton in the dark suit, Florence Harman in the purple coat, Messrs Whitehead to the right).* As runners up in the Amateur Cup Final, this was United's finest hour – to date.

"This was my first ever Chesham Utd game and 49 years on I am still watching with unbound enthusiasm, usually for next season! I remember Kenny Kent missing the penalty, but not really understanding the significance. Last season's win at Bristol Rovers is probably the closest the mighty Chesh have come to repeating the glory, along with the FA Cup 3rd round appearance. Up the Generals!" *Derrick Williams* MBE, *founder of KitAid, 2017.*

(With thanks to 'The History of Chesham United' written by Peter Gibbins in 1998).

Tennis

297. **The tennis courts at Chesham Bois Manor,** home to the Garrett-Pegge family until 1978. Like cricket and golf, lawn tennis began as a game played by the leisured classes. The rules of tennis owe much to Chesham's John Hinde Hale, who lived round the corner at Germains House in Fullers Hill during the 1870s. He was one of the six founding members of the All England Club at Wimbledon and is credited with the invention of the rectangular tennis court and serving areas that we know today.

298. **Chesham Lawn Tennis & Croquet Club** was established in 1879 on land opposite Germains House owned by Squire John Fuller. It remained there for almost 100 years. Since 1976 the Club has been based at Pednormead End and for many years has offered both squash and tennis courts. Grass courts and croquet lawns are resigned to history.

Tour de Pednor

301. **'Biggles',** also known as Kim Payne, sets off at lightning pace through Pednormead End in 1982.

299. **Roy Castle,** who presented TV's 'Record Breakers', from 1972, and for over 20 years until his untimely death, saw fit to leave his Gerrards Cross home to lead the way during the 1982 Tour de Pednor – which remains, of course, to be Chesham's premier annual sporting event! Participants gather at the Queen's Head pub in Church Street and tackle five gruelling miles around the Pednor Loop.

300. **Winner Tim Atkins,** pictured two years earlier, shares his glory with Richard Penrose *(right)*.

302. **James Gilbert and 'Big Phil' Holmes** *(right)* tend to technical difficulties during the Tour of 1980.

Chapter Ten
The End

303. **A very early photograph of St Mary's Church**, c.1860. The graveyard, now enclosed, must once have extended into the grounds of The Bury and Lowndes Park, as burial remains have been found there. The first written record of the church is dated 1220, and the earliest built evidence of its origins is the arch of an 11th century Norman window. It is likely that a wooden church would have predated this, and the pudding stones in the current foundations suggest a place of worship which may go back to the Druids and pre-Christianity. What is clear is the fact that very many generations of old Chesham families, going back at least one thousand years, lie buried under the small hill on which the church sits.

304. **The Will of Hannah Hawkes** of Chesham, dating from 1720.

"If we have had a long and useful life we may like to tell of it on a tombstone. 'She was endowed with every virtue that could grace the woman and adorn the Christian in every situation of life' are the words on the tomb of Laetitia Law, buried in Chesham, 1842.

Gravestones, or tombstones, followed fashions, and before the 17th century there were very few. The typical tombstone would face east to west and be aligned with the church. The headstone would often be paired with a footstone which was often much smaller and normally had the initials of the deceased with their year of death. In some cases a bodystone would sit in between."

Clive O'Sullivan, who has recorded the remaining tombs in St Mary's churchyard and restored the Trinity Baptist churchyard memorials. See facebook.com/cheshamlocalhistory

"Sawdust spread thickly on the roadway indicated a severe illness in a nearby house, to quieten the noise of the horses' hooves and the wheels of the carts, and if death followed, the big black hearse, with glass sides, would come out, pulled by a pair of glossy black horses."

Kathleen Winifred Flory (née Webb) 1909-1994

Death & Spirituality

305. **Chesham Cemetery** opened in 1858 on Honeysuckle Field and Asprey's Orchard, when the churchyard at St Mary's Church was declared full. Originally there were two chapels, two lodges and several outbuildings including a hearse house. There is consecrated and unconsecrated ground and, since 1967, an area for Muslim interments.

(See the booklet '150th Year Celebration of Chesham Cemetery' published in 2008 by Chesham Town Council. A book 'Faith in Chesham' is currently being compiled by Neil Rees.)

306. **The great oak tree,** on Marvel Hill at Dungrove, must be well over 200 years old. In recent decades it has become the site of ceremonies, meditations, the scattering of funeral ashes and, as a sign of the times, a place of pagan and spiritual symbolism.

307. **The Spiritualist Church** in Higham Road. This is a non-denominational church based on spiritual healing and on receiving communication, through a medium, of proof of the continuation of life. It has been an active church, also known as a 'sanctuary,' since 1932. Amongst its supporters were the Rev Walter Wynn of the United Free Church and his son-in-law Harry Bates, who was also a headmaster at Germain Street School. Both had been profoundly affected by the death of their sons from war and illness.

THE GOOD EARTH

Sweet song of bird and drone of bee
Pink blossoms on an apple tree,
The fresh green scent of new-mown hay,
The pearly hush of dawning day,
Incense of roses after rain
Or honeysuckle in the lane,
A rippling stream, a clear blue sky,
A breeze that sings a lullaby,
A field of poppies in the sun,
Ripe corn, it's harvesting begun,
A baby's smile, a loving word,
Tree, flower, stream, and child and bird
Make glad my contemplative mood,
For then I know that God is good.

A poem penned by Eva Rance, who was born in Chesham in 1906, and whose memoirs were published as 'Eva's Story' in 1991

Celebrating Life

"The overtly religious and sombre funeral ceremonies, typical of the Victorian era, are becoming increasingly rare, and there is a rise in civil celebrancy and woodland burials. The value of these is in the sense of connection between the loss of a loved one and the natural passage of time. The psychology of being grateful for and celebrating a life is a powerful tool for the ongoing health and wellbeing of those that remain".

"This book of old photographs is not designed as a lament for Chesham's past, but as a celebration of the town as it continues to grow and transform. Our purpose, as residents of Chesham, must be to guide the town towards change for the better, by working with those who govern it, by taking responsibility for our own everyday actions and attitudes, and by serving one another".

Peter Hawkes, August 2017

Photographic Sources

Ray East Collection 1, 2, 6, 8, 10, 15, 17-22, 30, 32, 34, 36, 37, 39-41, 43, 45-47, 67-70, 72, 81, 87, 88, 90-92, 94, 96-98, 100, 106, 107, 109-111, 114, 116, 119, 121-126, 131-143, 145-149, 151, 154-156, 159-161, 165, 171-173, 185, 187, 189-193, 196, 197, 202, 205, 209, 213-217; 222, 223, 225, 227, 228, 233-235, 241-245, 261, 262, 264, 265, 269, 286, 292, 297, 303; Peter Hawkes 4, 5, 7, 31, 33, 71, 76, 84, 93, 95, 99, 101-5, 108, 115, 120, 130, 152, 153, 175, 182, 183, 186, 194, 195, 204, 236-8, 248, 250, 256, 293, 294, 298, 305, 309, 310; Ben Brotherton 9; Kathryn Graves 11; Kathleen Libra 12; Paula Western 13, 14, 257; Donald Dixon 16, 28, 77, 78, 85, 166, 170, 226, 295, 296; Phil Cox/Stan Cox 25, 168, 169, 259; Ray East 26, 27, 79, 80, 210, 211, 212, 224, 249; Terry Cherrill 29; Ann Barwell 38, 57, 267, 276, 277; Tina Reading 42; William Hughes 44; White Hill Centre 48, 51, 288; Paul Marchant 50; Derek Naismith 52; Vanessa Robinson 53, 299-302; Chesham Grammar School 55, 56, 58; Chiltern Hills Academy 59; Keith Fletcher 60-65, 89, 174, 246, 247, 254, 272, 274, 275, 279, 282; Ray Edmunds 66; Peter Sadler 73, 74, 308; Colette Littley 291; Bagnall Centre 82, 83; Phil Webb 86; Anne Crabbe 112, 251; Ian Freeman 118, 270, 271, 307; Marie Knight 127, 298; Stuart Lloyd 128; Michael Wright 144; Syed Kamran Mustafa 150; Pam & Stephen Cheeld 157, 158; Mimi Biro c/o Val Biro 164; Alan Cross 176; John Hutchinson 177; Roy Turner 178; Chesham Town Talk magazine 181, 289; c/o Tesco plc 184; Ray Williams JPS 199, 200, 201; c/o Fizz Hitchcock (presumed to be the photographs of A J Scrivener 218, 229, 230, 231, 260, 266, 273, 290; Sue Gordon / Chesham Museum Research Group 219; Paul Collins 220; Ian Newton 221; Michael Peppiatt c/o Michelle Sage 223; Carl Jones 232; Alan Linger 239; David Page 240; Mark Barnes 255; TT Boughton / Chesham Library 263; Roy Marron 268; Chess Vale Bowling Club 278; Chartidge Park Golf Club / Eric Roca 280; Peter Gibbins 281, 283; Cliff Davies 284, 285; Jean Podbury 287; National Archives 304; Albert Braithwaite 306; Maura Hawkes 311.

Acknowledgements for assistance: Richard Hughes, Sophie Honeybelle, Hilary Povey, Ian Newton, Chesham Museum staff, Matt Kirby, Hugh Hawkes, Maura Hawkes, Amy Deane, Keith Fletcher, Christian Schwetz, Masud Ahmed, Mark Crow, David Roden Mansell, Clive O'Sullivan, Natasha Newlands, Jon Channer, Mary Casserley, Michelle Sage, The Buckinghamshire Examiner, Neil Rees, Jonny Ellis, Vicky Carling, Donald Dixon, Fizz Hitchcock.

308. **A few paintings** by Peter Sadler *(above is Chesham station)* and George Bridges *(front cover, chip shop fire in Waterside)* appear in this publication. They have both produced many more of the town.

309. and 310. **The earliest photographers** in Chesham were William Butts and William Coles, who were trading in the late Victorian era.

Other Publications in the Series

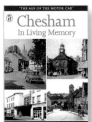

Chesham in Living Memory

P Hawkes & P Cox

Find out how the town developed from the 1940s through to the present day due to the demands of the motor car and the unstoppable age of progress. Heavily illustrated with photographs through the decades. An interesting focus on both architecture and motor vehicles.

£9.95

Pubs & Inns of Chesham & Villages

R East, K Fletcher & P Hawkes

A fascinating guide to the historic public houses of Chesham and district, including more than twenty establishments that are still serving today. Featuring over 100 alehouses, inns, taverns and beer shops in the town centre and the surrounding Buckinghamshire villages.

£12.95

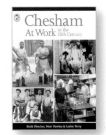

Chesham at Work in the 20th Century

K Fletcher, P Hawkes & L Perry

A history of the main sectors of trade and manufacture that provided work and a livelihood for Chesham people through the 20th century. A celebration of Chesham's industrial heritage, and a portrait of its workers and the many varied items that they produced in the town.

£12.95

Further details from:

Hawkes Design & Publishing Ltd
2 Laceys Yard, High Street, Chesham, Bucks HP5 1BU
Telephone: 01494 793000
Email: phawkes@btconnect.com
www.facebook.com/cheshamheritage

FOR THE FULL RANGE OF BOOKS GO TO:
www.hawkesdesign.co.uk

Peter Hawkes was born in Chesham in 1966 and his family can be traced back to the beginning of the town's parish records of 1538. In a Chesham charter he discovered an individual called Hugh Hawkeshead, born about 1220. Peter has two children, Maura and Hugh.

311. **Portrait by Maura Hawkes**

Surname Index

Call for More Stories

Want to inspire another book? If your family's story is worth telling and has not been included, or if you have spotted an error/omission, or if there are any photographs of the town between 1860 and 2000 that you would like to submit, please do get in touch. There are 1,000s of images stll to publish in the Ray East Collection. They just need your stories as captions. Look out for the next publication!

Write to:

Peter Hawkes, Director, Hawkes Design & Publishing Ltd
2 Laceys Yard, High Street, Chesham, Bucks HP5 1BU

Email: phawkes@btconnect.com